# PLAIN TALK ABOUT THE WORD BUSINESS

Robert Flannes
Philip Geyelin
Robert Alden
Creed C. Black
James S. Copley
Art Buchwald
Elmer W. Lower

Robert M. Goshorn
Joseph J. Famularo
Walter B. J. Mitchell
E. J. McCabe, Jr.
Chester Kerr
Alfred C. Edwards
F. L. Rodgers

# PLAIN TALK ABOUT THE WORD BUSINESS

Rex Goad
Mori Greiner
Karl Fleming
John Steele
Arthur Rothstein
Gilbert Grosvenor
Arnold Gingrich
Robert Stein
Al Silverman
Robert Brown
John B. Babcock
James W. Michaels
Dennis Flanagan

Walter A. Stalter
Donald H. Hunt
Edward G. Freehafer
Bill M. Woods
Dan Seymour
Whit Hobbs
Thomas B. Adams
William Bernbach
Jerry Fields
Thomas Dillon
Bert C. Goss
Roger A. Ross
William Weilbacher

PUBLIC AFFAIRS PRESS, WASHINGTON, D.C.

ACKNOWLEDGMENTS

This book is the outgrowth of a series of articles originally published by the Yale Daily News under the editorship of Andrew P. Garvin, Daniel H. Yergin, Scott Newman, George Priest, Philip Garvin, and Lawrence Bragg. In a very real sense what follows is the fruit of their labors—their judgment, resourcefulness, and imagination.

Special thanks is due E. Donald Elliott, Jr., present publisher of the Yale Daily News, for permission to reprint the articles included in these pages.

The articles by Messrs. Freehafer, Gingrich, and Steele are adaptations of writings by them previously published by the New York Life Insurance Company, the Magazine Publishers Association, and Dodd, Mead, and Company.

In the course of preparing this volume for publication, Public Affairs Press has benefited considerably by the generous cooperation of the authors and the assistance of Walter Wheeler and William Markley.

M. B. SCHNAPPER
*Editor, Public Affairs Press*

Copyright, 1970, by Public Affairs Press
419 New Jersey Avenue, S.E., Washington, D. C.

Printed in the United States of America
Library of Congress Catalog Card No. 72-112291

# INTRODUCTION

### By John Hersey

There would be no sausage business were it not for pigs, alas for pigs, no sardine-canning business but for the fish in the sea— and no "word business" without words. Words have to be strung together somehow before they can be said to have become valuable for either commerce or art, and the writer is the only one who can bestow this value. Without the writer all the book and newspaper publishers, broadcasters, telecasters, magazine editors, advertisers, librarians, critics, literary agents, lecturers on *belles lettres,* theatrical producers, booksellers, and sundry hangers-on and parasites of the "word business" would be thoroughly out of business.

What does it mean to be this one without whom . . . ? What *is* a writer? Perhaps a good approach to an answer is to try to define what it does *not* mean to be a writer.

It does *not* mean lying in a hammock with the filtered sunlight dappling a sybarite's ecstatically motionless figure. This is a common popular picture of a writer: a man who does nothing. Nothing, except perhaps occasionally late at night, probably while under the influence of alcohol or drugs. If he stirs his lazy bones in the daytime, it is only because inspiration has fallen on him in his hammock, like a dropping from a bright-plumaged bird in the boughs overhead. . . . No, that picture is false.

It does not mean getting rich. Not long ago the Authors League of America conducted a survey of professional writers and found that their average annual income from free-lance writing was about $3,000. Changing times and changing dollars will have revised that figure upward somewhat; but it is still brutally true that for the average writer, whether he be scholar, *avant-gardiste,* romancer, philosopher, poet, reporter, or hack, wealth is not the reward for his labors. Headlines about the very few who hit the jackpot (and that image from the one-armed bandit is apt, because the slot machines of the word world toss their infrequent jackpots out in the most unlikely disorder, to Mickey Spillane and Katherine Anne Porter, to Harold Robbins and Saul Bellow)—such headlines give the public, and also give many would-be writers, another false picture: of Croesus at his typewriter. No, in order to support themselves and their families, most writers resort sooner or later to moonlighting,

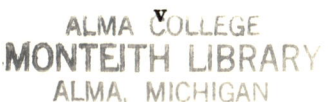

and the most common form of moonlighting, paradoxically, is writing itself—working, that is, somewhere in the "word business" described in this magazine; the next most common form of moonlighting is teaching.

It does not mean doing things "at your own pleasure" and "on your own time." Most writers, even most of the most gifted of them, write to deadlines of one sort or another—some of them self-imposed. The word "deadline" has an earnest ring, for it means: If you cross this time-line without a finished and workmanlike manuscript under your arm, you're dead. If not of starvation, then of oblivion.

It does not mean fainting with pleasure at the sounds of the world's praise ringing in the ears. The world's praise, or even the praise of a very small circle, is chary and fickle. There is nothing more dangerous to a writer than to have it, for in the very moment of his turning his head to hear it more sweetly, it runs and grows cruelly coy or makes off for good.

Then what *does* it mean to be a writer?

The reward of writing is in the writing itself. It comes with finding the right word. The quest for a superb sentence is a groping for honesty, a search for the innermost self, a self-discipline, a generous giving out of one's most intimate rhythms and meanings. To be a writer is to sit down at one's desk in the chill portion of every day, and to write; not waiting for the little jet of the blue flame of genius to start from the breastbone—just plain going at it, in pain and delight. To be a writer is to throw away a great deal, not to be satisfied, to type again, and then again, and once more, and over and over. It is to ring changes, not repeat, not fall onto a dead center.

If one is to search out the real meaning of being a writer, a warning has to be stated in the context of this publication. If the basic impulse has to do with commerce, with making a killing, then the would-be writer should beware. He will never make it. The underlying and sustaining impulse is, and must remain, quite different: It is the impulse to tell someone something—to offer, almost as to someone to whom a letter is being written, a set of appeals to the senses, of pictures and sounds and smells and tastes and palpable tactile feelings, and another set of appeals to the mind, subtle and keen, and finally, binding the rest together, a set of appeals, unsentimental yet compelling, to the emotions. He must want to pierce reality with his personal vision and tell someone else what he has seen.

## ABOUT THE AUTHORS

JOHN HERSEY, master of Pierson College at Yale, once worked for Time, Life, and The New Yorker. His novel "A Bell For Adano" won a Pulitzer Prize.

ROBERT FLANNES is director of personnel of the Los Angeles Times and president of the Newspaper Personnel Relations Association.

PHILIP GEYELIN, formerly diplomatic correspondent for the Wall Street Journal, is the editor of the editorial page of the Washington Post.

ROBERT ALDEN, an assistant editor on the New York Times, has covered stories for the Times in Europe and Asia.

CREED BLACK is former managing editor of the Chicago Daily News.

JAMES S. COPLEY is publisher of the San Diego Union and chairman of the Copley Newspapers.

ART BUCHWALD is a columnist of the Washington Post Syndicate.

ELMER LOWER, president of ABC News, was formerly chief of the CBS and NBC Washington news bureaus.

REX GOAD, director of NBC News, has covered sixteen national political conventions.

MORI GREINER is general manager of the Scripps-Howard radio station in Memphis, Tennessee.

KARL FLEMING is Newsweek bureau chief in Los Angeles.

JOHN STEELE, Time-Life Washington bureau chief since 1958, previously worked for United Press in Chicago and Washington.

ARTHUR ROTHSTEIN, technical director of Look, is also a member of the faculty at the Columbia School of Journalism.

GILBERT GROSVENOR is vice president and associate editor of the National Geographic Magazine.

ARNOLD GINGRICH is publisher of Esquire Magazine.

ROBERT STEIN is vice president of the McCall Publishing Company and former chairman of the American Society of Magazine Editors.

AL SILVERMAN is the editor of Sport, a Macfadden-Bartell magazine.

ROBERT BROWN is the fiction editor of Esquire Magazine.

JOHN W. BABCOCK is president of the American Business Press.

JAMES W. MICHAELS is the editor of Forbes Magazine.

DENNIS FLANAGAN is the editor of Scientific American.

ROBERT GOSHORN is secretary of the Central Registry of the Magazine Subscription Solicitors.

JOSEPH J. FAMULARO is vice president for personnel relations of McGraw-Hill Incorporated.

WALTER B. J. MITCHELL, JR., is vice president of the Dell Publishing Company.

E. J. McCabe, Jr., is the president of Grolier Incorporated.

Chester Kerr is director of the Yale University Press and president of the American Association of University Presses.

Seth Agnew, former president of the Children's Book Council, was the manager of Doubleday's books for young people.

Alfred C. Edwards is the president of Holt, Rinehart, and Winston.

F. L. Rodgers is secretary of Charles Scribner's Sons.

Walter Stalter is publications manager of the Itek Corporation.

Donald H. Hunt is deputy director of the Free Public Libaray of Philadelphia and recruitment chairman of the Council of National Librarian Associations.

Edward G. Freehafer is the director of the New York Public Library.

Bill M. Woods has been executive director of the Special Libraries Association.

Dan Seymour is president of the J. Walter Thompson Company.

Whit Hobbs is senior vice-president of Benton & Bowles Incorporated.

Thomas B. Adams is president of Campbell-Ewald and chairman of the American Association of Advertising Agencies.

William Bernbach is chairman of the board of Doyle, Dane and Bernbach Incorporated.

Jerry Fields is a director of Jerry Fields Associates.

Thomas C. Dillon is president of Batten, Barton, Durstine & Osborn Incorporated.

Bert C. Goss is chairman of the board of Hill & Knowlton Incorporated.

Roger A. Ross is an advertising and production writer for the Smith, Kline & French Laboratories.

William W. Weilbacher is director of research of the J. Walter Thompson Company.

# CONTENTS

### I: NEWSPAPERS

| | | |
|---|---|---|
| *1:* | Opportunities in Journalism — *Robert Flannes* | 1 |
| *2:* | The Reporter's Trade — *Philip Geyelin* | 7 |
| *3:* | The Foreign Correspondent's Lot — *Robert Alden* | 12 |
| *4:* | Anxieties of the Managing Editor — *Creed C. Black* | 16 |
| *5:* | The Publisher's Role — *James S. Copley* | 19 |
| *6:* | How To Be A Columnist — *Art Buchwald* | 23 |

### II: BROADCASTING

| | | |
|---|---|---|
| *7:* | Television News — *Elmer W. Lower* | 27 |
| *8:* | Wedding Words and Film — *Rex Goad* | 30 |
| *9:* | The Reasons For Radio — *Mori Greiner* | 35 |

### III: MAGAZINES

| | | |
|---|---|---|
| *10:* | Reporting For News Magazines — *Karl Fleming* | 41 |
| *11:* | Covering Washington — *John Steele* | 46 |
| *12:* | Telling the Story With Photos — *Arthur Rothstein* | 51 |
| *13:* | Pictures and Words — *Gilbert Grosvenor* | 55 |
| *14:* | Words Will Always Count — *Arnold Gingrich* | 58 |
| *15:* | The Art of Editing — *Robert Stein* | 64 |
| *16:* | Sportswriting — *Al Silverman* | 66 |
| *17:* | Appraising Fiction — *Robert Brown* | 70 |
| *18:* | Specialized Publications — *John B. Babcock* | 72 |
| *19:* | Writing About Business — *James W. Michaels* | 76 |
| *20:* | Writing About Science — *Dennis Flanagan* | 79 |
| *21:* | Distribution Problems — *Robert M. Goshorn* | 83 |

### IV: BOOKS

| | | |
|---|---|---|
| *22:* | Success Between Covers — *Joseph J. Famularo* | 89 |
| *23:* | The Paperback Revolution — *Walter B. J. Mitchell, Jr.* | 94 |
| *24:* | Textbooks and Reference Books — *E. J. McCabe, Jr.* | 98 |
| *25:* | Scholarly Publishing — *Chester Kerr* | 102 |
| *26:* | Publishing For Children — *Seth Agnew* | 106 |

27: The Business Side — *Alfred C. Edwards*   110
28: Challenges and Opportunities — *F. L. Rodgers*   114
29: Implementing Ideas — *Walter A. Stalter*   118

### V: LIBRARIES

30: Providing Information — *Donald H. Hunt*   125
31: Service For the Community — *Edward G. Freehafer*   127
32: Specialized Fact Finding — *Bill M. Woods*   130

### VI: ADVERTISING

33: The Idea Business — *Dan Seymour*   135
34: The Creative People — *Whit Hobbs*   140
35: The Prospective Ahead — *Thomas B. Adams*   144
36: The Way You Say It — *William Bernbach*   149
37: Fact, Fiction, and Money — *Jerry Fields*   156
38: The Account Executive's Responsibilities — *Thomas Dillon*   159
39: The Public Relations Side — *Bert C. Goss*   164
40: Sales Promotion — *Roger A. Ross*   169
41: The Backbone of Research — *William Weilbacher*   174

# I
# NEWSPAPERS

# 1

## OPPORTUNITIES IN JOURNALISM

### By Robert L. Flannes

Editor? Reporter? Sports editor? Political writer? Entertainment editor? Foreign correspondent? Business editor? Copy reader? Publisher?

Why not? Careers in these job classifications and many others are realistic possibilities for the young men and women who are seriously interested in journalistic careers in the newspaper field.

How high can you go in newspapers? The question must be answered by a question. How willing are you to work hard, continue your learning process after graduation, and dedicate yourself to one of the most rewarding careers possible?

Employment opportunities on the news and editorial staffs of newspapers are greater today than they have ever been. And all signs point to increasing opportunities—particularly for those young men and women who have acquired knowledge through formal education, who recognize that learning doesn't cease upon graduation, and who have a desire to fill an exciting and responsible role in the most challenging field of all—communications.

Some persons (mostly in competing media) have claimed that newspapers are already dead or are in the process of dying. Any change in newspaper ownership, no matter what the reasons, leads to all kinds of dire predictions about the future of newspapers.

Such premature burials, however, completely overlook the facts. Stanford Smith, general manager of the American Newspaper Publishers Association, shed some impressive light upon the true situation while addressing a conference of the Newspaper Personnel Relations Association several years ago.

In 1947, Mr. Smith pointed out, newspapers employed fewer than 250,000 persons. By October of 1965, newspapers employed more than 350,000. This was a 40 per cent increase in about 18 years. This increase, Mr. Smith said, towered over the 25 per cent rise in all types of employment and the 10 per cent increase in all manufacturing employment during this same period.

The increase in newspaper employment is all the more significant because it occurred during a period when major technological improvements and automated processes created significant changes in the methods of producing newspapers.

In 1965, Mrs. Smith reported, daily newspapers in the United States and Canada spent more than $140,000,000 for plant expansion and modernization. This was the sixth successive year over $100,000,000. Hardly a dying industry!

Of at least equal importance, and it may be deserving of even greater weight by the college student who is approaching a career decision, is the increased emphasis by newspapers upon upgrading the quality of their news and editorial staffs. Journalism has changed dramatically in the last decade, and all signs point to a continuation of change.

A survey report released by the Newspaper Personnel Relations Association early in 1966 developed some strong indicators of how these changes are having a favorable impact on employment opportunities.

Over 200 newspapers participated in this survey which was concerned with the recruitment and training of editorial department employees. At the time of the survey, 48 per cent of the responding newspapers said they had openings for reporters, and over 59 percent said they were trying to hire good copy editors and copy readers.

Most newspapers reported that they were having more difficulty than in previous years in finding good people to fill these jobs, and 51 per cent expected even more difficulty in the future.

It would appear, therefore, that there will be a continuing demand for bright young people in newspaper journalism. The career opportunities are plentiful.

But, you may ask, are newspapers willing to pay competitive salaries? Or do they expect high quality talent to work for newspapers for considerably less money than that same talent could draw working for other media or in the public relations field?

Here again, the outlook is good and constantly improving. Publishers recognize that better salaries are needed to attract and retain the better talent. And in recent years there has been a decided upgrading in journalism salaries.

Most published salary figures for positions in news and editorial departments have been concerned with so-called "starting salaries" or with Guild contract rates for reporters, etc., which are usually referred to as the "scale rates." In both cases, the published figures represent minimums, and they do not reflect the actual amounts above the minimums and above the scale rates that are paid by newspapers all over the country as a general practice.

This is not to imply that editors and publishers have suddenly lost their heads and that they are paying fantastic rates to the beginning journalist just because he has his college diploma. Editors and publishers are realistic. They try to pay people what they are worth. They are buying talent, and they pay well for proven talent.

The new college graduate, however—even the graduate with his master's degree—is not a proven talent in most instances, and he is expected to show by his own actions what he can do rather than rely entirely upon his college degree.

Salary patterns in the newspaper business follow the same general pattern of salaries in other types of businesses. There are significant geographical variations, there are differences between the small town and the big city, and, most importantly, there is a definite relationship between salaries and size of newspaper as measured by circulation and by gross annual revenue.

Starting salaries for beginning reporters are subject to many variables. Whereas, the average starting figure currently may be around $100 per week for a beginner, factors such as geography, size of newspaper, educational background, extent of training and experience usually determine the specific rate for the individual beginner.

The minimum starting salary in some cities is around $125 weekly, and editors may hire talented beginners well above the reported minimums.

What is the best preparation for a career in journalism? Must the young man or woman be a journalism school graduate, or can a liberal arts graduate do equally well over the long run?

Certainly, the product of a good journalism school, who has had experience working on his school newspaper and who perhaps has had a summer or two as an intern on a newspaper is going to possess highly desirable qualifications which should make him attractive to most newspapers.

But this does not mean that a liberal arts graduate with a desire to become a newspaper man can't also gain acceptance and a chance to progress. Many editors hold to the premise that they can teach journalism to their new employees, but they can't educate them and, these editors are just as impressed by a good educational background as they are by a journalism degree.

The ideal combination, many editors claim, is the liberal arts graduate who has gone on to acquire a graduate degree in journalism.

The NPRA Survey referred to earlier found that 98 per cent of those newspapers doing campus recruiting did so among journalism majors. Students in other majors were not overlooked, however, and 83 per cent of the newspapers doing campus recruiting reported their recruiting also included students from other majors such as English, political science, etc.

It must be pointed out, while mentioning campus recruitment, that newspapers as a whole have not been as aggressive in these activities as have many other types of businesses. Unfortunately, therefore, the true story about career opportunities in newspapers has not been extensively presented on college campuses.

The college student considering a journalism career can profit by thorough investigation. Get out and talk with the editors of newspapers in your area. Visit the small dailies and weeklies as well as the medium-size and largest metropolitan newspapers.

A high share of daily newspapers operate intern programs. Explore this possibility. A summer or two in a newspaper's intern program will help you form your decisions about your journalism career. This experience also will make you a more valuable beginner when you do start full-time employment.

Talking and associating with experienced, successful newspaper journalists will convince you that this field offers plenty of opportunity for the well-educated person who is willing to work for success.

You will also learn that there is a feeling of excitement, of responsibility, of continuing challenge, and of self-satisfaction in doing a good job—a public service type of job—in helping your fellow citizens learn about and understand what's going on in the world around them.

## 2

## THE REPORTER'S TRADE

### By Philip Geyelin

Go West, young man, and keep going. You, too, can build a reputation, overnight, in Saigon.

Not too long ago, that might still have been sound counsel for the young, would-be newspaper reporter, bent on making it big in a hurry and eventually becoming a national correspondent, ideally in Washington. For the gambler with good instincts, it might still work —though probably not in Saigon.

When a relative handful of bright young reporters were working the Vietnam war story just a few short years ago, it was the rarest of journalistic motherlodes. It was a burgeoning crisis, unrecognized, sorely under-reported, badly misunderstood, and endowed with an American Embassy whose approach to information-giving was so lamentably inept that every twist and turn of U.S. policy or strategy was almost automatically suspect.

The war was ready and waiting for the crusading, eye-catching expose. Awards were soon showered upon the few fortunate, talented, hard-digging young men who then had Vietnam to themselves.

The key words are "fortunate" and "few." These are now several hundred American correspondents covering the Vietnam story, and at least a dozen of them are more seasoned, better-balanced, and more competent all around (though less celebrated, alas) than the young men who made the first big strike. Sheer competition alone sharply reduces the chances of a tyro making it big, fast, in Vietnam now.

There is one consolation in all this, however, though some might consider it inadequate. Early, sudden success and instant acclaim are not always the surest auguries of a long career as a newspaper reporter. All too many reporters (in the very strict sense of the word) are enticed from the highest calling by the lure of fame or monetary reward or prestige into television, bookwriting, or punditry.

Having recently written a book, and abandoned what I considered one of the best reporting jobs in journalism (as Washington diplomatic correspondent for the *Wall Street Journal*) to cast judgments from the editorial pages of the *Washington Post,* I should know.

To the argument that this might disqualify me as a commentator on the lot of a reporter, I would answer that the fallen (after almost 20 years) may sometimes have a better perspective on the true faith.

In any case, the sudden celebrity, with the good fortune to have a near monopoly on expertise in some subject of rising concern, is that much more likely to succumb all the earlier to television's glamor; to The Book; to the allure of a column; to the far darker temptation of becoming a party to the action and—in the name of reporting—of allowing opinion to distort the recounting of events. There is an honored place for punditry and there are no good pundits who are not good reporters too.

So much for the glory road. It is not knock against those who are smart and lucky and talented enough to find it, to observe that a career founded upon doing so is a career unsoundly founded. It is almost a contradiction in terms.

A good reporter's lot, by and large, is not likely to be a happy one if professional happiness is equated with either fame or fortune.

Most of the good reporters in Washington are good, in part, because they are relatively unsung. Or perhaps they are unsung because they are good—because they regard the accurate, unvarnished and unsensational recital of events or facts or atmosphere or appearances as the highest calling.

Faithfully done, it ought to be as much a public service as elected office, or tax collection, or delivering the mail or garbage disposal. It is that rich in its variety, that indispensable, and more often than not, that unglorious.

The hard-knocks road can be much more quickly dismissed. It is the temptation of almost all eminent grey-beards in the trade to dramatize their rise to eminence by dwelling most heavily on the difficulty of the club.

"Get yourself a good grounding, my boy," was the advice of one distinguished elder, when I had the temerity to ask him if he had any openings for a beginner in Washington. "Five years with a good, small-town newspaper is what you need," he went on. "You can't understand this town, until you understand City Hall."

Maybe so, but cross-examination revealed that this particular greybeard was one of those rare exceptions who had made the big jump to Washington at the start. You'd be surprised how many "exceptions" there are.

If you want to be a reporter, and don't feel keenly about plying the trade on the national or international scene, then the home office of any good newspaper is a good place to begin.

But if you are really intent on covering national or international news, there is a certain logic in trying to start out where you want to be, and no insurmountable barrier to doing so. There are no clear-cut rules of procedure, to be sure. But there is something to be said for simply being on the spot, in almost any capacity, as long as it offers opportunity to shop around.

The turnover in Washington news bureaus is considerable, which puts a premium on knocking on the right door at the right time. This, in turn, means being in the neighborhood, and in an environment which might produce the timely lead.

More than ever, education matters, in journalism itself, or in special fields. Anthony Lewis of the *New York Times* demonstrated what a year's study of law can do for Supreme Court coverage. The same rule applies as well to economics for the Treasury, physics for the Space Administration or political science for politics.

But chance, and persistence and anything else you might have working for you are—and always will be—critical elements. The way to become a columnist, Stewart Alsop is fond of recounting, is to have a brother who already is one.

So what have you got, when you've got it? We have ruled out fame or fortune, and need not dwell overlong on such bromides as hard work, bad hours, deplorable working conditions.

One thing you've got is management in all shapes and sizes, from publishers to top editors to the copy desks. Charitably, all these can be thought of as allied trades, if not necessarily as allies. Publishers should be revered, if only because the reporter is nothing without machinery, paper, ink and some sort of wage. Editors can help as well as hound, hinder or harass—or all in combination.

In any case, it is a large part of a reporter's lot to have to learn to live with no end of counsel, some of it sound, most of it unsolicited, and just about all of it beyond effective dispute. A reporter, in the scheme of things, very rarely has the last word.

But he does have, for all this, an opportunity to practice an art form of a sort while performing a service essential to democratic, self-government—and all this in the best of company and from a ring-side seat on events both large and small.

A typical day, for a typical Washington correspondent, is almost certain to combine drama with drudgery. There will be wasted motion, then suddenly rich reward.

The scene (for a man not nailed down in one of the big bureaus to a single beat) can shift abruptly from the Bureau of Labor Statistics to the President's oval office, from an all-but-empty Senate Chamber to a hastily-assembled background briefing at the State Department on a critical turn in world affairs, from a noisy, crowded diplomatic reception to the panelled office of some high official who knows what he is talking about and is not afraid to talk brilliantly about it to a reporter he trusts.

Any good story requires the patient assembly of some dry hard facts—rice production in the Mekong Delta, rainfall in India's wheat-growing areas, the rise or fall of consumer prices, and what pushed them up and down.

But there are also bright moments among the long hours of enforced idleness. Some years ago I spent a whole day sitting in a hotel corridor with a dozen determined colleagues for the privilege of finally seeing John L. Lewis emerge from eight hours of hard bargaining with the coal operators and hearing him render, after a melodramatic pause, his own version of "no comment," when asked for a progress report.

"Gentlemen" he intoned, "There is no balm in Gilead." Whereupon, refusing to elaborate, he stalked away.

With the right credentials, you could have crouched in the locker-room in an Abilene, Kansas, high-school football stadium, taking refuge from a driving rain-storm, as the only reporter lucky enough to have sought that particular haven, and listened to General of the Armies Dwight D. Eisenhower arguing with a confused clutch of amateur advisers about the relative merits of delivering his first campaign speech for the Republican Presidential nomination in the dry confines of a locker-room, for television, and without an audience, or outside in a pelting rain.

Lacking a consensus, the General suddenly tired of the aimless debate around him and, with a curt "Damn it, let's go," led the way outside.

Or you could stamp your feet in the snow, and watch John F. Kennedy put together, bit by bit, the New Frontier from the doorstep of his Georgetown home.

Mostly, what you have is a license to be a detective in a continuing who-dun-it—or perhaps a who's doing-what-to-whom—and why. Now and then momentous stories are dished out for self-serving purposes —and reputations are made.

Most of the time it's a question of asking the right question, at the right time, of the right source, who is quite often somebody who is unhappy about what's going on. To find that somebody, in itself, requires a considerable grasp of what *is* going on.

The big scoop aside, some of the best reporting is a piece-work affair, a painstaking business of assembling many elements, from many sources, adding a little deduction and some sound judgment, about big and little things, under pressure of the keenest competition anywhere in the world.

That it can be hectic and require hard choices, even in the little matters, is illustrated by the plight of columnist Rowland Evans, when it was suddenly borne in upon him, as he began lunch with Senator Jacob Javits in the Senate dining room, that he had made a conflicting engagement for that very moment for lunch at a men's club several miles away with Senator Eugene McCarthy.

Evans weighted all his options and swiftly decided to sit through the soup with the Senator from New York, who had moved only a few steps from his office to keep his engagement, and take the main course with the Senator from Minnesota, who had, after all, made the larger effort meeting him downtown.

If it is hectic, sometimes, it is almost never dull to be dedicated.

Even the careful recital of an Agriculture Department crop report or a highly technical analysis of a trade agreement is of urgent consequence to someone, and as vital as a State of the Union address to the proper understanding by the governed of their government.

In the last analysis, this must be the basic source of satisfaction for the reporter, and the best justification for his not-always-happy lot.

# 3

## THE FOREIGN CORRESPONDENT'S LOT

### By ROBERT ALDEN

The trade of foreign correspondent is an esoteric one, not to be undertaken lightly.

The foreign correspondent becomes accustomed to sitting on his valise under a hot sun at some deserted airport, with no transport, no hotel room, no one in sight who can speak any known language. He thinks no more of such a plight than he did when as a cub reporter he got lost in Brooklyn while in pursuit of New York Supreme Court Justice Samuel S. Liebowitz.

The foreign correspondent gets adjusted to living out of a suitcase and under a mosquito net. He gets used to telephones that won't work and chauffeurs who vow on the Koran that they know where they are going and wind up hours later apologetically shrugging their shoulders, acknowledging that they are hopelessly lost and counting on the foreigner to find the way home.

The foreign correspondent gets accustomed to waiting, waiting for hours to get entrance visas, waiting for permission to exchange money, waiting for permission to see the Prime Minister, waiting for permission to leave a country, waiting for permission to get permission.

A foreign correspondent learns to live without the amenities—without a glass of ice-cold water on a hot day, without a seat on the 50-yard line on an autumn afternoon, without the kind of chicken soup that mother used to make, without a copy of the Sunday *New York Times*.

One popular definition of a foreign correspondent describes him as a reporter with amoebic dysentary.

If all this sounds grim, then you're not cut out to be a foreign correspondent. You have to want to ply this trade with a deep conviction because it means giving up a good part of all that you have grown accustomed to through the years of your development. It represents a considerable sacrifice. But if you are willing to make this sacrifice, if you are willing to abandon the shores of home, then you have the first quality of a good foreign correspondent—drive, the drive to do the job and do it well.

You must also possess a handmaiden of drive—curiosity. You must totally involve yourself with knowledge of the country to which you are assigned. You must want to talk about it and ask questions about it endlessly.

It is not only a question of what foreign policy Prime Minister X tends to follow, but what has been the background of Prime Minister X, where does he come from, what have been the frustrations in his life. The foreign correspondent must know the economic condition of all segments of the population. He must know what the educational system is like, what scientific progress is being made in the country, what does a farmer eat, what does the workingman do for recreation, what are the religions, what are the prejudices, what are the fears.

The correspondent must saturate himself in the life of the country he covers. In an age of specialists, there can be no specialist among good foreign correspondents, for the good correspondent should be able to understand and report on anything that happens in his country, anything from a badminton match to a revolution.

A good correspondent should be able to match his curiosity with an ability to tell his reader 12,522 nautical miles away what is going on and in terms that the reader will understand. That is not as easy as it sounds. There are different frames of reference, and the correspondent must continually keep in his mind's eye the frame of reference of the reader 12,522 nautical miles away.

He must see things as that reader would see things, be startled by things that would startle the reader and be able to explain those things in ways that will strike that reader. Thus the crush on a Jakarta bus could appropriately be described for the New York reader as being "like the subway at the rush hour if people were permitted to cling to the outside of the cars as well as cram themselves inside."

The foreign correspondent should not be the sophisticate. He must instead be perpetually searching, perpetually seeing the country he covers and its people with a fresh eye, perpetually surprised at things that might not even be of interest to the jaded foreign correspondent but would, in fact, surprise the reader who had never left his easy chair in an American living room.

A foreign correspondent must also be what we describe in the newspaper trade as a "self-starter." A reporter who works in the city will be told by his editor to go out and cover a fire or a sewer pipe scandal or a speech by the Mayor.

But the foreign correspondent is 12,522 nautical miles from his boss. He must make his own assignments. If he has to be prodded, he is not a good foreign correspondent. His boss cannot possibly know as much about what is going on in a country as the man on the scene.

Illustrative of this is the fact that when we give an assignment to one of the several good foreign correspondents who happen now to be working on the *Times* city staff, he will come back with the story he covered and perhaps a half dozen more. A good foreign correspondent is like a vacuum cleaner sweeping an area clean of anything that will be of interest to his reader. He is not happy unless he is filing stories, one a day, two a day, even more.

A good correspondent should, of course, have done some spadework before he goes out to cover a particular area. But I don't feel it is necessary to do this spadework at college or graduate school. Several weeks of intense reading and interviewing at the United Nations and in Washington should give the reporter a good base on which to begin his venture into a new land.

Language facility is important although, depending on the country, it is not always crucial. It would be unthinkable for anyone to try to cover France without a good knowledge of French. But, in Southeast Asia, for example, nine major languages are in use and it would be a rare foreign correspondent who could understand more than a smattering of many of them.

Fortunately English is a key language in most parts of the world. French is often useful, as is Spanish, and the correspondent with a particular interest must be prepared to undertake the difficult job of learning Russian, Chinese or other such specialty.

In my view, I would much rather have a good reporter without language facility than a poor reporter with great linguistic ability. One of the best of all foreign correspondents speaks no language save English and speaks that imperfectly due to a speech defect.

The point is that the stock in trade of the good foreign correspondent is an ability to overcome whatever difficulty presents itself and that includes weeks away from one's home base and one's family, housing difficulties, bureaucratic barriers thrown in his path, intimidation, threats.

The good foreign correspondent, ever hungry for a good story, is ready to move toward the scene of a story as an almost automatic reflex. It is not something that can be taught. It is in the bones of a man. If you have to weigh the decision as to where you stand, you're probably not foreign correspondent material.

# NEWSPAPERS

What are the job prospects for the would-be foreign correspondent?

There are fewer men representing newspapers overseas these days, with the exception of *The New York Times,* which has 37 full-time correspondents on overseas assignment and 144 others on a part-time basis. But the press associations, Associated Press and United Press International, have large staffs overseas, as do the news magazines, such as *Time* or *Newsweek.* The number of radio and television correspondents has increased greatly in the last 25 years.

The *Times* usually recruits its foreign correspondents from within its own ranks, from our own local and national reporters who have demonstrated ability and have the desire to work overseas. The news magazines and press associations usually follow the same policy.

Occasionally, although not on the *Times,* someone already overseas is hired on the spot. Thus there is a breed of adventurous young men who take the chance. They go to the scene of a big story—the Berlin wall or the war in Vietnam—and they try to get a job once they are there. It is a risk. But for the man with a deep desire to be a correspondent it is a risk worth taking.

How much do you want to be a foreign correspondent?

Try this test. At 5 o'clock one morning I found myself walking in a light rain through the streets of Tokyo. I was on my way to the office to file a story after a night of roistering. Almost all of Tokyo was asleep except for the noodle vendors who ply their trade in Tokyo all through the night. I had on a trench coat. My hands were plunged deep inside my pockets. I had a good story to write, and I was sublimely happy.

If you would be happy in similar circumstances, then you will understand that all the sacrifices mean nothing. You could be a foreign correspondent.

# 4

# ANXIETIES OF THE MANAGING EDITOR

## By Creed C. Black

What's it like to be the managing editor of a big city daily?

The answer depends on the timing of the question. There was one frigid day in the winter of 1966, for example, when I was ready to trade jobs with almost anybody else on the staff. Counting noses, I discovered that the *Chicago Daily News* had:

Two men in Los Angeles, one taking over our bureau there and another—his predecessor—showing him around.

Two men in San Francisco on an assignment they had suggested.

Two men in Honolulu with President Johnson.

One man in Miami covering a spicy murder trial.

One man in Sarasota enjoying the sunshine with the White Sox.

One man on his way to Long Beach with the Cubs.

Meanwhile, I was sitting in my office watching it snow when my secretary walked in for approval of an expense advance for two staff members—presumably the only ones left at home—who were setting out on a little expedition to investigate vice in the bars at company expense!

It was a moment to make me appreciate a comment by a reporter on a paper where I had worked earlier. This reporter had taken a call from the president of a civic organization who wanted the newspaper to send a representative to a meeting but who preferred "nothing lower than an editor."

"Sir," the indignant reporter replied, "there is nothing lower than an editor."

But the seasons pass. The sun is shining again in Chicago as these lines are written and I can bask not only in it but in the reflected glory of a poised performance of a competent and courageous staff during one of the most hectic news periods any of us can remember.

A vacation now beckons, and during it I can look back on a summer in which we covered racial violence, mass murders, space flights, elections, an escalating war, an airline strike, an inflationary economy and—for welcome relief—a White House wedding.

This is not, of course, the kind of news I would choose to live with day after day. Rather, it is the kind of news which helps explain why a University of Illinois psychologist said he had found that newspaper editors and writers have the highest anxiety level of any United States professional people studied—higher even than Navy underwater demolition experts or aviators in training!

But our task is to report the world as we find it, not as we wish it were. It is to produce what another editor once described as "a work of art, a daily attempt to reduce the chaos of the universe to some kind of order."

The role of the managing editor in all this is never the same from one day to another. And probably on no day is it ever what first Hollywood and now TV would have you believe.

I can remember shouting, "Stop the press!" only once in my life, and that was not because we had just outwitted the police and solved the crime of the century but because we had left in a story an erroneous paragraph which supposedly had been killed.

On the *Daily News,* our chain of command begins with the editor, who is responsible for the total editorial product. The associate editor answers to him for the editorial page and the managing editor for the rest of the non-advertising content of the paper. We have two assistant managing editors—one for news and one for features—and roughly a dozen department heads.

With eight editions a day and a publishing cycle that runs from 8:30 a.m. to 6:15 p.m., no one can see everything that goes in the paper. I read as much of it as I can—or at least scan it—after it's in, so I won't be embarrassed by someone who calls or comments personally on something we've published.

But that's a heavy diet of reading, and the inability to keep up with it—plus all the other reading that should be done—is one of the frustrations of the job. Time, in fact, always seems to run short in this business. There are more meetings to attend, letters to answer, readers to placate, job applicants to interview, production problems to solve, memos to write and stories to plan or check than there are hours in any day.

That, however, is not a problem peculiar to the newspaper business. And the solution here, as elsewhere, is to develop a strong organization, delegate responsibility and concentrate on policy, planning and personnel. Even so, an editor must stay close to the news if he is to be effective in influencing the way his newspaper covers it.

For that reason, I try to spend most of the morning in the newsroom going over the first edition and discussing the outlook for the rest of the day. Then at the end of the day our department heads meet in my office to talk over the prospects for the following day and beyond. And at night I stay in touch by phone when necessary.

If it doesn't add up to the Hollywood stereotype, it is all the same a stimulating and satisfying career which I cheerfully recommend.

Despite the dwindling number of large metropolitan papers, the newspaper business generally is a growing profession with a bright future. It needs intelligent, professionally trained young people to grow with it.

As modern life becomes more complex, the need for improved communications becomes all the greater. In terms of the newspaper, that means a need for skilled people who understand contemporary events, who can report and interpret them accurately, and who can use the facilities of modern journalism wisely.

And speaking of the facilities of modern journalism, it should be added that technical advances in the field of communications do not necessarily make the search for and dissemination of truth easier.

With the advent of television, we have seen the advertising experts move into the field of public affairs to merchandise a political candidate or a point of view with the same techniques they use in selling soap and toothpaste. The responsibility of newspapers to give the people the information and perspective they need to form their own —and more critical—opinions thus becomes heavier instead of lighter.

The rewards of a newspaper career, I believe, can be great. Salary levels have been steadily rising for a number of years and are continuing to rise; they will go higher as more well-trained people enter the newspaper profession—and stay in it.

And I can say from experience that there are in this field, as in few others, rewards that cannot be measured in strictly economic terms. Prestige is one. The sheer pleasure and the excitement that linger after the daily frustrations are forgotten are others.

Finally, there is the highly satisfying sense of accomplishment that comes when you tuck that paper under your arm and head home with the feeling that you've devoted your day to something worthwhile.

# 5

## THE PUBLISHER'S ROLE

*By* JAMES S. COPLEY

A newspaper must have a respected place in its own community. In fact, my kind of newspaper is one that is recognized as a symbol of community leadership and responsibility.

A good newspaper serves as the conscience of the public. It reflects the image of its community through selective news coverage and wise editorial counseling on community projects and problems.

My kind of newspaper devotes its most immediate interest, news and comment to the local community. In this connection, let me paraphrase E. W. Scripps, who directed his newspapers from Miramar in San Diego County. He said that what the public knows it learns through the community newspaper, and whatever the beliefs or bias of the community's mind, it is largely the result of what is read in the newspaper.

I expect—the community expects—some pretty difficult things from any publisher.

First of all, loyalty is expected. A publisher must fight for his town. If his town needs something, he must try to get it. It may be a new bridge, or a new industry, or a more efficient government.

This brings us to the second thing which is required of a publisher. That thing is patience. Just as Rome wasn't built in a day, neither is the average city. And haste makes waste in anything. This is why our newspapers don't start great "crusades" too often. We would rather work 52 weeks a year, instead of one or two weeks a year, for the things we believe in.

The third thing a publisher needs is tolerance. He works with a lot of honest people who have a lot of honest differences of opinion about what a city needs. He must try to help all these people go in approximately the same direction—the direction of real and permanent progress.

The fourth thing—perhaps it is the first thing—a publisher must be able to do is make a profit. A newspaper that cannot make a profit is going to have a loss, and a newspaper that has a loss is bound to skimp on machinery, or on brains, or on editorial coverage.

Back at the turn of the century, some newspapers didn't see the importance of the linotype machine and they didn't save up the money to buy one or two. As a result, they finally couldn't compete. They died, or they were sold. They were silenced, not by censorship, but by bad financial judgment. So it is the job of a publisher to keep solvent, and keep modern.

How does a publisher go about making a profit? He makes it by giving a service—a service in which no one can match him. He makes it by being a newspaperman, gathering news, seeing that it is delivered to people waiting at homes or on street corners, people who in turn read the advertisements that help him pay the salaries necessary to go on with the news-gathering and the news-printing.

It sounds simple. It isn't simple at all. There is no more demanding job than being a newspaper publisher, whether the newspaper be in a large or small city. In fact, it is likely to be a tougher job in a smaller city.

In a great metropolis, the burden of being a publisher is eased by the presence of staff assistants, specialists of many kinds, which is made possible by much greater financial resources. In a smaller city, a publisher may have to play both the piano and the drum, and between times saw on the violin. Sometimes he may feel like the original one-man band.

He is not a one-man band, however, and that is part of his problem. Sure, he himself probably can write an editorial. Sure, he can sell an ad. Chances are, he can even set a stick of type. He may even be able to substitute on a newspaper delivery route.

But the hardest thing a publisher may have to do sometimes is tilt back in his chair, and let other people do the writing and the selling, and just think of ways to help them do it more effectively.

A publisher has to work with more varied kinds of talents than almost any other businessman. And he has to pretend to be as smart as any of them.

That goes for the reporter, who has a creative mind; it goes for the advertising man, who may be both a writer and a salesman; it goes for the people in the complex mechanical departments; it goes for the people in circulation, and those in accounting. They are all specialized experts, and he has to be almost as expert as any.

The hardest thing he may have to do is to let them alone, as individuals. His job is to help this group of individuals work as a team, and to carry the ball himself on major decisions.

But the publisher has to keep his eye on things—all kinds of things. He has to see that the editorial department has a healthy respect for spelling names right; that the circulation department doesn't miss cancassing a new section of homes; that the composing room meets its deadlines with regularity; that accounting keeps him posted on even the smallest changes in operating margins.

All the while the publisher is also trying to feel the pulse of his community and of his staff. He is a busy man, you see—and I have not mentioned what may be his biggest job of all.

This job is to be a force of continuity in his community—someone who stays on his civic job even when others leave or are retired. Mayors and councilmen come to the ends of their terms, the publisher's appointment is indefinite.

The publisher has too look to the future, 10 or even 100 years away, when his newspaper will still bear at least part of the responsibility for progress of the community.

This being the case, he has to be a conscience of the community. He must try to satisfy himself as to what is right or wrong.

And because his community is part of a greater community—the county, the state, the nation—he must try to express himself in the decisions of all of these. Sometimes he will do this in editorials whose ring, he hopes will be heard in the state capital or as far as Washington.

Sometimes he may find he has to be unpopular because he tells truths as he sees them. He knows, however, that if he is honest, people will credit him with this. And they won't stay mad very long.

In fact, something else will soon come up, and they may seek his counsel. Whenever a community has a problem, the publisher is soon consulted. The graver the problem, the sooner the call may come. And if he is a good publisher, he is like a fire brigade—he is ready for the summons.

Sometimes he may find he has to be unpopular, because he tells truths as he sees them. He knows, that if he is honest, people will credit him with this. And they won't stay mad very long.

The publisher of a community newspaper is asked to be a fire department, ready for his community's call; he is asked to be a circus master, of many different kinds of talents; he is asked to be a writer and a paper boy and an ad salesman and a printer, but one who can still desist and watch the others do their jobs; he is asked to be a magician, and keep more money coming in than is going out despite all the rising costs that hit all businesses; and he is asked to be a good eater of chicken or steak at many, many meetings, when he might sometimes rather be home with a glass of milk.

The Copley Creed uses other words which say what I mean: "The newspaper is a bulwark against regimented thinking. One of its duties is to enhance the integrity of the individual, which is the core of American greatness. Each city in which we publish is a city of distinctive personality. Each newspaper must be a distinctive newspaper reflecting the life of each hometown. No one can think for the American people. We believe it is our responsibility to ring out the truth loud and clear, and to stimulate thought at the close personal level of the individual and the community."

6

## HOW TO BE A COLUMNIST

*By* ART BUCHWALD

The first thing you must learn if you're going into journalism is never to write a free article for a college newspaper on what it's like to be a newspaperman.

When somebody asks you for a 1000 to 1500 word article describing some aspect of your work in the publishing world, write back that you will be happy to do it for $1000 to $1500 depending on the circulation of the publication.

There is a tremendous likelihood you will never hear from the school again.

If they agree to your terms, then you can go into some nonsense about what a great business journalism is and what great rewards it holds for those who love the printed word, etc., etc.

The truth is, I haven't the slightest idea about how to go about being a columnist.

I know you have to lie to get your job. At least I did—told the editor of the *Paris Herald Tribune* I had six years newspaper experience. I figured he wouldn't check the references, and I was right.

You have to steal. No newspaperman can live on his salary. So you have to make it up on your expense account. Most of the creative writing in journalism today is being done while newspapermen make out their expenses.

You don't have to be a strong drinker to be a good newspaperman. It may help you think you're a good newspaperman, but booze and writing don't go together as well as they used to.

Most of the successful newspapermen I know are sober, and it's usually the ex-newspapermen who are holding up the bars.

"Yeh, I know. But how the hell do I get to write a column?"

Once again I have no idea how you get to write a column. I started out writing about night clubs in Paris. Then I started interviewing people. Finally I said to the powers of the *New York Herald Tribune*, "You're wasting this stuff in the European Edition. You better syndicate it before it's too late."

They did, and it's a great life except when I get a letter from some college asking me to write a piece for them about my career.

All right, this is how I operate.

I don't speak to anyone.

Facts get in my way.

I read the *Washington Post* and the *New York Times* in the morning, and then I write a piece which takes 45 minutes. The rest of the time I play gin rummy, ogle pretty Washington secretaries or write articles for college newspapers and magazines.

I am very happy in my work. I don't like competition, and I don't encourage anyone who thinks he would like to start a similar type of column.

I have no advice for anyone except to stay out of my racket if he knows what's good for him.

I guess that about does it.

If you stick with it, and work hard and lon ghours and marry the publisher's daughter, you'll get your own column in no time at all.

# II
# BROADCASTING

7

## TELEVISION NEWS

*By* ELMER W. LOWER

Why has television become the average American's primary and most trusted news source?

According to a poll by Elmo Roper Associates, the majority of Americans not only get most of their news from television, but rate TV more believable than newspapers.

One reason for this is that the news departments at the three networks are unique among all media in that they edit news on a daily basis for the nation. Our editors can judge each story for its impact on and interest to the people of the entire country—not just the residents of a particular locality.

No daily newspaper enjoys the same luxury. Economics forbid it. When the *New York Times* tried to launch a Western states edition a few years ago, it proved a dismal failure. Advertisements were few. *Local* news was limited. As a result, the *Times* went nowhere, proving, I suppose, that as in New York, people in the Far West buy newspapers for the advertisements, the local society reports, the sports page, and the comics, as much as for the news. Yet the *Times*' venture was a noble one. It was an attempt to fill a void left by too many newspapers in this country: namely, the failure to cover properly world and national affairs.

If I can make a prediction, I would say that this continued failure will probably make network television even more firmly entrenched as the public's number one news source.

Our dynamic and mobile society is also a major factor. For instance, a college man in New Haven who watches the Frank Reynolds-Howard Smith program and reads the *Times* will still be able to watch the newscast in every state of the union when he graduates. But when he moves outside the Northeast, he'll have to develop a loyalty to another newspaper. And whether that newspaper will be up to the standard of excellence to which he's accustomed is doubtful. Chances are, he'll wind up picking his local paper primarily on the basis of how much it tells him about the city or town in which he's living. (Newspapers are very much aware of this trend. It's no accident that the growth publications today are the suburban dailies which concentrate on community news.)

What concerns me in this whole situation is that the American public may feel that by watching television news exclusively, it can consider itself well informed. Nothing could be further from the truth.

We in television news are the last ones to feel that we are the sole news medium. At the present stage of our development, we're limited by time to reporting most stories in a few well-chosen words or pictures. We don't pretend to give an exhaustive analysis of every move in the Vietnamese War, or the reasoning behind every Presidential decision, or in-depth reports on the political climate from Spain to Japan. Any given night we might touch on one of these subjects. But not all at once. And not as completely as we would like. Only half hour or hour documentaries fill that need. Indeed, I sometimes wonder if even that is enough. Several years ago ABC devoted an entire prime-time evening—three and a half hours—to a program on every aspect of life in Africa north and south of the Sahara. Yet, even in that time we barely scratched the surface.

So, at the present time, the intelligent viewer should and must supplement his television news viewing with careful reading of a responsible daily newspaper (if he's lucky to be near one), and magazines and books.

I said "at the present time." All three television networks now present thirty minutes of news each night, and a good many documentaries each year. This volume has grown in recent years rather markedly, and will continue to do so, in my opinion. Robert E. Kintner, to whom we are indebted for the development of NBC News, has suggested that the day is not too far distant when one or more networks will present an hour of news each night—and in prime time! I agree with him. The fact that many stations now supplement the network programs with substantial local news programs is, of course, a step in the right direction.

Marshall McLuhan may call me a traitor to the cause of visual information, but I don't think the printing press and its products are on the verge of extinction. They are complementary to broadcast news. And if anything, they're more necessary now than ever before, because the amount of news that's vital to the American citizenry is immense. I think that radio and television news inspire the thoughtful viewer to read more.

So, I think it's safe to say that no matter which phase of the word business a student decides to enter today, there's little danger that he'll find himself working for an obsolete medium in ten or twenty years.

Newspapers—magazines—broadcasting . . . they'll all still be here. Perhaps there'll even be a few new ways of distributing information. But in all of them, the challenge will still be the same: to explain a thoroughly confusing world as clearly and intelligently as possible to an increasingly well-educated, inquisitive public.

# 8

## WEDDING WORDS AND FILM

### *By* REX GOAD

Television news is in its infancy. It is without precedents except for those established in its few years of existence. It offers dimensions to be found nowhere else in journalism, and its role is constantly expanding and changing with the continuing technical improvements and innovations.

Yet in all basics the television newsman must acquire the same knowledge of news work as the journalist in any other medium—newspaper, wire service, news periodical. He must start with that experience, or in a position where he can acquire it under sound news direction, then progress from there to a knowledge of extremely complex technical factors.

His ultimate purpose is not really different from that of the newspaper man—and newspaper or wire service experience are excellent assets—but, to translate his facts and words into a report for the public, he must master complicated tools. He must wed words to live events or to film or videotape.

In effect, he must serve an internship and residency before he undertakes the role of a specialist. There are not yet enough such experienced specialists, and only now are people beginning to fully appreciate how specialized this realm of journalism is.

I do not think it is a career for which a student should shop around. I think it beckons to and requires some inherent traits, such as an incessant hunger for knowledge of the world, society, politics, human motives. It requires persons who find fascination in reading, both for content and for discovering how writers make words do vivid and exciting things. It requires persons who believe events, all events, are important and that it is important that the public be told about them. It requires persons who have an abiding enthusiasm for news work, as fresh and unjaded after forty years as it was when they left college.

We have spoken of specialization. Television newsmen and women may pursue several avenues within the news organization with which they work.

# BROADCASTING 31

Some may seek to become writers on so-called documentary programs; some may guide themselves toward the role of producers; some may be copy editors who get their sense of fulfillment out of improving the writing of others; some may cover wars and riots in the street; some may become critics or commentators who work principally from studios.

Actually more than two-thirds of the large news staff of the National Broadcasting Company does not go on the air at all but edits, writes, produces, assigns, administers. This is also true of ABC and CBS, but in individual stations a far larger proportion does occasional air work. Yet in all the categories the same experience background is an essential to the best ultimate results.

The job opportunities are endless for both the experienced and those just entering their careers. Expansion of news programming has been going on, both from the networks and the individual stations, for several years. News programs of fifteen minutes have been extended to thirty minutes and then to one hour.

Every step in this process creates personnel needs, and the process will continue with technical innovations, such as satellite transmissions. The networks, more and more, reach out to the individual stations for experience and skills, and the stations, in turn, go to the colleges for the new people who in a few years will be running the whole show. Strong news operations are a critical essential to television stations everywhere, a situation which will not change.

The transition from life on the campus to a career is difficult. It always has been. Television news, however, is one of those professions in which there is short supply of persons with discernable potential.

There was a time in the news world, before television, when a substantial formal education was not so basic a requirement. The world has changed too much, too fast for this to be any longer true. Self-education can be very effective, but it takes much longer than the college years, and we live in a world of competition and impatience.

This does not mean that formal education for journalism requires courses in a journalism department. Some of these are excellent but the essential factors remain a broad general education in what are usually called the arts and sciences—literature, writing, languages, political science, economics, history, basic sciences. A time is upon us when more specialized reporting is important, and a thorough knowledge of one subject is an asset in news.

Courses in a journalism school can be extremely valuable to the student who intends to make news a career. It offers him the gratification of working in the element of his choice, but more important it provides him with some practical knowledge of the particular technical elements involved. It even can sharpen his knowledge of the use of words.

In brief, the journalism course gives the student some initial contact with practical problems he will encounter in his first job and, as such, is a blue chip to be placed on the desk of the personnel man who interviews him for a job.

It may be an entirely personal conviction, but I have a suspicion that sometimes the "activities" man on the campus is serving personal vanities more than matters of substance. I once asked an electioneerer why he thought I should vote for his man for student president. He said: "Because he plays in the band and they like him!"

We are dealing here with the career of a newsman. He certainly might profit from membership in a debating society or other activity involving public speaking. He most certainly can profit from work on student publications or in college radio or television stations. And if he is seeking summer employment, he should go to the newspapers, the wire services or the radio-television stations—where what he does can fit into his patterns of experience.

If he wishes to engage in campus politics, he should do so with a view to learning some of the political axioms. As a general rule, the proper journalist must be capable of full detachment, if not absolute objectivity. And what is "objectivity" anyway, except another term for open-mindedness or perhaps simple maturity—so rare and so essential to a complete journalist

I still have the subjects of salary and a time-table of progress to deal with, both of them painful. Salaries are the poorest of all avenues to examine in determining whether one wishes to devote his career to news. They vary greatly in different regions, but they are much better than they were a few years ago. Even the man of limited talent who can perform an essential journalistic function can expect to support himself, and later a family, in some decency.

I suppose on the average the starting pay is around $110 to $135 a week at individual stations, give or take. They are higher at the networks, where reasonably substantial initial experience is required. But these are the minimums, and those who reach the fullest flowering of their talents as correspondents and producers reach incomes well into the upper brackets. There are all sorts of intermediate stages, but it is reasonable to say that television newsmen of ability are well paid.

It was noted earlier that the television journalist must start with the same basic news knowledge common to newsmen in all media, including the ability to cover stories accurately, and to write. Television correspondents do not read copy written for them but are required to write their own. There are too few good writers despite the fact that the ability to write and the desire to do so should be regarded as a minimum requirement.

I know of no yardstick to measure the speed of advancement, once a news career is started, any more than I know of a yardstick to determine how successful a skilled journalist may be on the air.

All we know is that the correspondent on the air must inform the public, he must communicate with the audience and we prefer that he be himself; that is, that he have a touch of individuality rather than an actor's tricks or an elocutionist's artificialities.

Many writers, some of whom reached heights of literary accomplishment, came out of the ranks of the journalists, back through the centuries. Many of them you know. A few, such as Stephen Crane, are particularly interesting to the student seeking new combinations of words which wil give vitality to even the commonplace. Read those authors. Read everything you can find which adds to your knowledge of the fascinating things which can be done with common, everyday words.

I may have left the impression that journalists are dedicated and cloistered persons given to missions and meditations on the meaning of devotion. On the contrary they are activists, sometimes so close to the raw nerves of events that it taxes their endurance. They should not be participants but observers and reporters; not joiners but detached outsiders.

Much of the news is unpleasant and dirty. Much news work is routine, exacting and exhausting. You will find that the public insists it wants the truth, but that what you found to be indisputable is challenged by members of the public because it violates their individual prejudices or their view of how the world should be.

Yet none of us is infallible. The ideal is to be sufficiently self-critical to discover one's own slips even before the intelligent dissenter identifies them. We are not privileged because we may be aware of a public trust; it is the public trust which is privileged. There is room for the instincts of a gentleman in the rough and tumble of dealing with the most sordid. The burden of conduct is on the newsman; if he cannot rise above the bad manners of the other person, his advantages are gone.

It's a very attractive career. But only if you are right in entering it, if you really know what you want to do. You will get out of bed daily with a sense of urgency and anticipation. And on your death bed you can say: "I lived. I know, I saw it all."

9

## THE REASONS FOR RADIO

*By* Mori Greiner

There are considerably more radios in America than there are people. There are 242,000,000 of them, in fact, and they are with us at work and at play, in sickness and in health, indoors and out.

Some stations to which those sets are tuned play specialized music. Some speak in foreign tongues. Nearly all of them broadcast time, temperature, weather reports, traffic conditions, sports scores, market summaries, advertising messages, news, commentary and opinion in an almost ceaseless flow; for radio today is a link to everywhere, to what is happening and what is about to happen.

It is ubiquitous, and listened to by three out of every four adult Americans every day; a statistic which demonstrates, perhaps better than any other, modern man's insatiable lust for companionship, his desire for diversion, his need to know.

That statistic also sums up the first of five reasons why radio offers a writer opportunities beyond belief.

Think about it for a moment. Try to comprehend the challenge and the glory of a communications system that is truly nationwide. Consider that the *New York Times* has a weekday circulation of 725,000, and compare that figure to the unduplicated weekly audience of more than 24,500,000 Americans who listen to NBC's "News on the Hour."

A writer must be "read" to be effective; he must reach people. And radio reaches people.

There are seven major radio networks in the United States, 6,260 individual stations, and more coming. This total number presents a second obvious opportunity to the writer: he can apply for work at 6,267 different places.

The sprawling structure of American radio offers a third opportunity, too, an important one which the novice often overlooks. In the parlance of performers, it gives him someplace to be bad.

Johnny Carson, Danny Thomas, Garry Moore, Jonathan Winters, and Jack Paar didn't spring fullblown from a 21-inch picture tube. No, Virginia, not even a black-and-white tube. Each of them began amassing his millions at the rate of $50 a week on a local radio station. So did dozens of other present-day stars. A job at the local station offers the beginning writer a similar chance to learn his trade, develop his personality, perfect his professional skills, and move upward and onward when he is ready to do so.

Talent is a passing parade. The successful station manager seeks out young talent, develops and utilizes it while he can, and smiles through his tears when it moves beyond him.

As the parade goes forward, it leaves vacancies which in their very variety provide a fourth opportunity for those who work with words.

The most conspicuous vacancy today is in the ranks of the talker, the responsibile personality who can converse engagingly, intelligently, and grammatically before a microphone. Talk shows are *in*, but it is somehow extremely difficult to find people who have the fluency, the breadth of background, and the good taste to handle them well.

The second great need is for news writers. In the news area, radio competes directly but not well with television and the newspapers. Yet radio has distinct advantages in speed and mobility. It can report from the scene on brief notice. It can employ shortwave links and telephone lines and portable recorders. The technical tools are available, but many of the workers are maladroit. Imagination, skill, and just plain caring-enough seem to be the ingredients missing from most radio newscasts, and the writer who can supply these can go far.

There also is a continuing need in radio for advertising copywriters. Every radio station seems to have at least one anachronistically named "continuity writer" grinding out copy for local advertisers who do not employ advertising agencies. This is often a girl on a quick career-kick between college and marriage. As she develops facility, she is likely to go on to an advertising agency where the work load is lighter and the pay envelope heavier.

So jobs in this area are constantly opening up for beginners, and they can be very good jobs for young people whose intentions are serious. Creators of commercials are much maligned, but only because they are often inadequate to the task.

No one is offended by a logical, persuasive, effective and well-presented advertisement; in other words, a good one. Its preparation requires hard work and specialized skill, and its consummation brings considerable satisfaction.

Documentary writers are in demand, too. Some of the larger stations and most of the networks produce documentaries on both a continuing and a special basis.

The documentary writer is four-fifths journalist and one-fifth dramatist. He must have patience, perception, logic, and flair. He must be a skillful editor and a polished writer. Obviously, there are not and never will be enough documentary writers to go around.

The new sound of the networks has brought comedy writers back to radio to script the five-minute monologues by big-name comics which are sprinkled through the schedule. And it has attracted a specialist new to the medium, the article writer who comes up with general-information essays on nearly any subject for delivery as social or pseudo-political commentaries under the title of *Emphasis*, *Dimension*, or *ABC Reports*.

If you can write, there's a place for you in radio. The aural medium is challenging, but it has great things going for it. Inflections of the human voice, for example, can give meaning to words far beyond the capability of printed punctuation.

Then there's imagination—the listener's imagination—the most powerful and wonderful tool available to a writer. The radio dramatist doesn't have to worry about the limitations of budget and credibility so harassing to his counterparts in the visual media.

With mood music, sound effects and dialogue, he can create in jig time a radioactive space monster capable of ingesting Columbus, Akron, Youngstown, Cincinnati, Toledo, and the eastern half of suburban and metropolitan Cleveland, including Gates Mills.

What's more, the monster that lives in the imagination is far more horrible than the monster you can see.

On virtually no budget, the radio writer can transport his audience to a World War I flying field in France, a street bazaar in Cairo, or a subway platform at Canal and Broadway. He can call out the Marines or roll back the Red Sea.

The secret is to forget about Confucius and the arbitrary equation he established. Remember, instead, that one word evokes a thousand pictures.

So far, we've outlined four reasons why radio offers special opportunities to writers: radio reaches vast audiences; radio emanates from 5,630 separate places of business; radio gives writers a chance to be bad on a small scale, and a chance to be good on a big one; and radio needs writers in at least six basic categories.

More important than any of the others is the fifth reason—that radio is "conjugatable": it *has changed, is changing, will change*. In evolving over a relatively short span of time through boom and bust, two major and two minor wars, a population explosion and massive competition from television, radio has developed nimbleness and agility, a remarkable fleetness of foot. It is responsive to the times.

Somewhere, this hour, at least one radio station is trying a new idea, or a new twist on an old idea. That is so during any hour of any day.

Therefore, the writer who doesn't like radio as it is now can have a hand in changing it. If he's bright, if he's capable, if he's gutsy, he can help make radio into what it's going to be tomorrow or the day after, and he can have the time of his life doing it.

# III
# MAGAZINES

10

REPORTING FOR NEWS MAGAZINES

By KARL FLEMING

"How much is your stuff changed around in New York?" is the question most frequently asked of correspondents who sweat and heave for journalism magazines such as *Newsweek*.

Sometimes the question comes from a fellow journalist (definition: a newspaperman with *two* pairs of pantaloons) who's simply curious to know how a news magazine works. More often it comes from a skeptical and sometimes belligerent layman who suspects that the news indeed is managed through some kind of vague but sinister conspiracy.

It's amazing, in fact, how often a reader or an interviewee will say with a conspiratorial wink: "We know you're a man of integrity and honest intent, but you can't fight those editors in New York who change everything around to suit themselves."

That's just so much bilge and blather, of course. Especially so at *Newsweek*, where it is a point of procedure and pride that correspondents have absolute local autonomy over their stories. They see proofs and/or have stories in which they're involved read to them over the telephone near deadline time when geography permits. If there is an off-key word or derailed fact, the reporter has the clout to have it corrected. And does so.

I can't speak with any authority on what goes on in the editorial bowels of the other leading newsmagazine—"Brand X," as we call it—but despite the largely anonymous appearance of *Newsweek*, we like to think of it as a reporter's magazine, with "New York," the editorial headquarters, being dependent upon its 75 correspondents in 24 foreign and domestic bureaus to discover stories and conceptualize and report them in such a way that the eventual writer and editor in New York serve as polishers and finishers rather than as flinty-eyed machinators who subvert and distort as part of some grand and evil design.

The basic format and philosophy of the news magazine preclude every story carrying the individual byline of a correspondent (a fact, by the way, that disturbs reporters used to having their names out there on page one every day or so), but to an increasing degree *Newsweek* tries to get names onto and into stories. Most of the critical sections (books, movies, music) are now signed.

And on stories in other sections of the magazine, where the correspondent has done an unusually inventive, imaginative and enterprising job of reporting, his name will be woven into the text. This is being done not to satisfy the egos of reporters but to convey to the reader the fact that there are respected, trusted and able reporters with names and faces out there in the provinces explaining what is going on.

To use an industrial analogy, reporters in our bureaus around the world serve as miners. Their job is to search our rich veins of journalistic ore, to descend into the pit with pick and shovel, and to emerge with the richest possible raw material. The function of the writers and editors is to smelt down this ore and then process it into razor-like sharpness and diamond-like hardness, to distill away —to change metaphors in midstream—all but the purest essence of a story.

This means that the magazine's reporters produce what in a newspaper back shop would be called a lot of "overset." The reporter in the field is not expected to write a finished story. In fact, since his function is to exercise the five senses for a writer in New York far removed from the action of the story, the correspondent is urged to over-report. His files should have a fleshy, Rubenesque quality— oozingly rich with concepts, description, anecdote, analysis, explanation, history, meaning, narrative and relevance.

At the risk of over-simplification, the role of the newspaper traditionally has been to tell what happened—yesterday. What *Newsweek* tries to do—and this to me is what provides a professional satisfaction that more than offsets the rarity of bylines—is to tell in rich and vivid language not only what happened, but why it happened, precisely how it happened, why it is significant or not, what it means—all described in lovingly infinite detail that makes words march out upon the pages in the way a drama unfolds upon a stage.

In the Watts riots of August, 1965, for example, reporters in the Los Angeles bureau of Newsweek filed more than 100,000 words to New York. Other reporting came in from Washington, Chicago, Atlanta, Detroit, Houston, and San Francisco (what did Watts mean in those places? What was the national effect? What did Watts portend for the nation?) In New York, three writers stitched

MAGAZINES 43

it all together for an eight-page cover story which in my view still, after all the millions of words written about Watts, captures the anguished drama and tormented anger of that palm-lined ghetto better than anything else written about it. In the joy of such triumphant moments as that, one can forget a byline and take pride and satisfaction in the end result—a brilliant story produced by highly-professional teamwork.

There is a reasonably widespread belief that New York editors create all of the magazine's story ideas, and that the bureaus merely respond, Pavlovian fashion, to impulses from headquarters. Many ideas of course are indeed generated out of New York. But far more stories have their genesis in bureaus such as the five-man one I head in Los Angeles.

The responsibility of the bureau is not only to "cover" its assigned geographical territory on obvious stories such as Watts or the Texas tower murders, but also to create, as it were, those stories (which the local news media probably aren't doing) that help bring alive, translate and characterize the peculiar qualities of one section of of the world for another. California, for example, has its own individual style and flavor—an increasingly pervasive one nationally, by the way—and it's the job of *Newsweek's* bureau in Los Angeles to ferret out those stories that colorfully express that flavor.

Three times a week, for example, each bureau submits to New York a list of suggested stories from its region, broken down by departments in the magazine. Here's an example from Los Angeles:

"Nation (or movies): Time was when a handful of powerful overlords ruled Hollywood, and any star who strayed into political activism or social protest was flirting with having his career killed. No more. The power in the film colony is now so diffused that performers have become relatively independent. And more and more of them are expressing themselves on all sorts of unaccustomed subjects.

"This week, for example, both Gov. Brown and Ronald Reagan will be backed up at political events by their separate posses of movie stars. Reagan is having a $100-a-plate banquet Wednesday, at which John Wayne, Tony Martin, Lucille Norman, Buddy Ebsen and Don Defore will perform. Brown is opening his Southern California headquarters Tuesday, and on hand to help will be Gregory Peck, John Forsythe, Gene Barry and Tony Franciosa. Suggest we do a piece on how the stars are out for Brown and Reagan."

That suggestion resulted in an interesting political story and a fascinating glimpse into the new sociological character of Hollywood.

The key word, I suppose, in *Newsweek's* style of reporting is detail, detail—the tireless gathering of that seemingly unimportant minutia that gives people and places vivid color and unique character. The same applies to language. We try to avoid paraphrases and partial quotes, for the reason that most people have their own flavorful style of talking, which when faithfully recorded in a story helps give them character as individuals.

For example, I once got a quote from Bobby Shelton, the Imperial Whiz of the Ku Klux Klan, in which he said: "Before we start giving these niggers jobs, they've got to start improving their own status quo." In that one superbly hilarious sentence, the whole character, intelligence and attitude of Shelton is crystallized. Much better, we feel, than dehumanizing Shelton and saying that "Shelton feels that before Negroes receive equal job opportunities, they must improve themselves."

In this regard, the best journalism short-course I ever got was from William A. (Wild Bill) Emerson, a freckle-bellied Southerner who'd become the editor of the *Saturday Evening Post* and was formerly a senior editor at *Newsweek*. (Emerson is famous, by the way, for leaping from the LBJ Special which covered the South for Kennedy in 1960, in a lot of Dixie villages, running over to the depot where country folk would be arrayed on benches chawing and whittling, and saying: "I'm Harry Johnson of *Time Magazine*. Henry Luce sent me down here to see what all of you ignorant red-necks are thinking about." Then he'd run, naturally.)

I was in New Orleans working on a press section story in April, 1962, when Emerson telephoned. The religion section, he said, was doing a story on a confrontation between Archbishop Joseph Rummel and an excommunicated female parishioner named Mrs. Una Gaillot over the school desegregation question on the archbishop's lawn.

A New Orleans reporter and part-time "stringer" for *Newsweek* had sent in a perfectly adequate file on the story, Emerson said. But he (Emerson) was right on deadline, and he needed just two questions answered.

"Number one," he said, "What does the archbishop's house look like? Is it wood, or stone, or brick? Is it Victorian with ivy on the walls? What kind of day was it? Was it balmy and overcast, or hot and muggy? What does the archbishop look like? Is he old and bespectacled or what? How did he walk when he came out of the house? Did he stride angrily? Or did he walk haltingly, leaning on a cane? How was he dressed? What is the walkway like? Is it concrete, brick or gravel What do the grounds look like? Are there oak trees and rose bushes, magnolias and poppies? Were birds singing in the bushes? What was going on in the street outside the grounds? Was an angry crowd assembled? Or was there the normal business traffic, passing by oblivious to the drama inside? What were Mrs. Gaillot and her friends wearing? Did they have on Sunday best or just casual clothes? What happened as the archbishop confronted Mrs. Gaillot? Was he stern and silent? Or did he rebuke her? What was the exact language she used?

"Now," he said, "question number two . . ."

Though somewhat overwhelmed by the onslaught of his questions, I hustled out and in a matter of a couple of hours had recreated the whole scene and hustled off a quick file to New York.

When the story appeared in the magazine, its lead two paragraphs read:

"It was a cloudless, languid spring morning last week when Archbishop Joseph Francis Rummel emerged from his two-story, red-brick residence in uptown New Orleans and unknowingly moved toward a uniquely dramatic confrontation. Dressed in a long, black cassock topped by a velvet-lined cape, carrying a black cane in his left hand, the 85-year-old prelate walked haltingly toward a tall white statue of Our Lady of Fatima. There, fifteen neatly dressed ladies, on an annual pilgrimage to the shrine, awaited his greeting.

"The gray-haired archbishop had just finished welcoming the group when Mrs. Gaillot, excommunicated by Rummel the day before for her attempts to block desegregation of the area's Catholic schools, came stalking past fifteen pickets who were protesting the desegregation outside the archbishop's garden. Marching onto the lawn, Mrs. Gaillot threw herself on her knees in front of him. . . ."

That best describes, I think, what *Newsweek* is up to from week to week, and what makes it exciting, challenging and rewarding to be involved in so-called group journalism.

11

## COVERING WASHINGTON

*By* JOHN L. STEELE

In 1630 the puritan leader, Governor William Bradford, set upon his task of writing "The History of the Plymouth Plantation," with a promise to write "In a plain style, with singular regard unto the simple truth in all things." Today, as in that less complex century, this is a noble dedication; one not so easy to achieve. And for the journalist in Washington it still serves as a just cause for his being here at all, as well as for his monthly pay check from the office.

My subject lies in the limited area of "The News Magazine and Washington." And this means, according to the official register of the Periodical Press Gallery of the United States Senate, some 400 correspondents reporting for more than 200 publications. The interest span of these publications runs from the cosmic to the parochial. The "American Brewer" has a correspondent in Washington. So has the "American Milk Review," the magazine "Motor Boating," "Quick Frozen Foods," and a publication called "The Tobacco Leaf." For what happens in Washington, in things large and small, affects the well being, the fortunes, and the very lives of all of our countrymen. Indeed, what happens here has the most profound effect upon all the world. For some magazines the news lies in a comparatively restricted area, let us say government price supports for grains subject to fermentation, or milk, or the latest findings of government scientists concerning the incidence of cancer to tobacco consumption.

As for us at *Time* and *Life*, our interests in Washington are exceptionally broad-gauged and lie, with differences in emphasis, within the totality of the interests of our magazines. First, and most importantly, we apply ourselves to the "Res Publica,"—the public business in Washington. And believe me, our curiosity in this area knows no bounds. Wars and threats of war, elections, legislation, diplomacy, the state of the economy and its future prospects, weapons development and disarmament. Yes, and price supports and problems of the tobacco industry, too, though not in the continuing sense of our brethren of the more specialized publications.

# MAGAZINES

From where I sit, ithe job of the news magazine, in the sense that *Time* is one, is very far from the more or less traditional newspaper watchword emblazoned at the top left hand corner of *The New York Times* each morning, and reading "All the news that's fit to print." That is a laudable and commendable goal. But our job is far different and in many ways very much more difficult. By its nature, the news magazine is limited each week to merely a small fraction of the wordage found every day in large metropolitan newspapers. Thus at the outset our job is vastly different. Involved is the requirement for a more sharply honed editorial judgment concerning what a weekly news magazine should, indeed must, print. The competition for space in the weekly news magazine is intense: competition among many stories inviting our attention, and indeed beyond that, competition among competing ideas and concepts, within individual stories themselves. What criteria is used then?

First, and most importantly, the weekly news magazine in Washington—and everywhere else, too—applies itself to the story of more than transient importance. What is really important beyond a one day's headline? That is the question we keep asking ourselves. A speech in the United States Senate may claim a three-column headline in the afternoon newspapers and 24 hours later likely will be forgotten. That is the kind of story in which *Time*, is *not* interested. But there may be a speech in the Senate which presents the germ of a new idea. That could be of vast interest to us, even though it may have received little attention in the daily press. Or it could, in this same area, be a speech effective in changing votes or mustering opinion beyond the Senate, or a speech representing a new administration policy, or one signifying a coming to front-and-center of an important new public personality. That, too, would be of intense interest to us.

We are fascinated by the making of public policy. We make no attempt to cover in our weekly magazine all developments in making public policy; for instance every bill, or even every reasonably important bill moving through the Congress. We seek in this area the news development of more than transient interest. And once our interest is focused, we want to know a very, very great deal about the matter. If it concerned a piece of legislation we want to know, of course, what's in the bill. But we want to know specifically whose ideas went into the drafting of the bill; what needs it will fill, how it will be administered. We want to know in a qualitative sense if it represents good public policy, or whether the reverse is the case.

We want to know how the bill was passed through the Congress. How effective was the Executive Branch of Government in mustering pressure to pass or defeat the legislation? Precisely who did what to whom in this regard? Were arms twisted? They were? Then by whom and to whom? What arguments were compelling, what strategems were used? What was said in the back office caucus preceding the vote and how effective was it? Was the President directly involved and if so, how? We like to think that while we may come early on a story, we certainly stay late.

And we demand this same kind of reporting in every field touching upon the public's business: in the tangled evolvement of foreign policy, in the government's role in education, in civil rights, in the administration of justice and the courts, and all the rest.

Beyond the area of public affairs lie those matters of less importance but matters which fascinate people. The hegira of Lady Bird Johnson to rural America hardly meant nation-shattering news. But it did give us a warm story of the First Lady in a setting of small towns, Mississippi river boats and ice cream parlors. We've called on Senators taking their differences to a tennis court for adjudication (the Democrats won); and we've studied such diverse subjects as the unpopularity of U.S. wars, the working of Medicare and Medicaid, and the ravages of Dutch Elm disease. And this is merely a brief cross section of reporting done in Washington.

Another area which concerns us is that which one might call the more cosmic area. The relation of man to his environment, the nature of his society, where he comes from and maybe even where he is going. Not long ago, this realm took a Washington correspondent where hippies dwell, and with work of others elsewhere resulted in a fine cover story on a portion of a new generation little understood and ofttimes scorned. It took another Washington reporter to a learned conference on sociological, medical and legal aspects of abortion, a subject until recently taboo in the public press.

My point is that Washington reporting for a news magazine is almost unlimited in scope, bounded only by our energies and the magazine's editorial decisions concerning its interests in a specific week.

Who does the work in Washington? We have 25 *Time* correspondents, ten *Life* correspondents and photographers, others working for *Fortune*, or for our Radio-Television Division. We have a total Washington staff of sixty. *Time* itself operates news bureaus from New York to Hong Kong and back again, employs 100 full time correspondents, and scores of local correspondents or "stringers" in all parts of the world. In Washington we operate on what can best be described as a flexible beat system. We staff the White House with two men, the State Department and the foreign embassies with two men; three men patrol Capitol Hill, one the Pentagon, two the sources of economic decision making such as Treasury, the Federal Reserve Board and the international banking community. One correspondent covers the Supreme Court and the Justice Department, plus the law in general. Another specializes in Latin American affairs, another in science, another in the civil rights movement, two in the news falling within the general area of health, education and welfare. Others are on general assignment. But it is a flexible system because our news demands are flexible, some weeks with more emphasis in one area, other weeks with our primary attention going elsewhere. Our military correspondent can—and has— covered a National Open Golf tournament; he plays himself. Our White House correspondent is totally at home reporting on the broader aspects of Washington society, and our senior State Department correspondent has worked a police beat story. Specialists, yes, but generalists too.

Finally, I would like to give you my answers to the two questions I am most frequently asked by audiences of journalism students. The first concerns the process of preparing a *Time* story for print. The second involves the sometimes astonished assertion that: "You're not really objective, are you?"

The stories which you read in *Time* are written in New York by a remarkably skilled group of some sixty writer-editors. The reason, in the first instance, is a simple one. The reportorial resources of The Weekly Newsmagazine are immense. The story each week on the Vietnam war, for instance, comes not from one man in one place. It comes from *Time* correspondents on the battle scene. It comes from our men in the important listening post at Hong Kong. It comes from Washington, from our reporting on the decision-making apparatus of our government. And it comes from other world capitals as well. We also have, of course, the resources of press wire services, the output of the academic community, books, other tools of our trade as well. Somewhere, somehow this mass of material must be refined and reduced to printable proportions. That is the job of the writer-editor working in New York. And finally the responsibility for top editing falls upon the Managing Editor of the magazine. Does this mean a wide disparity between the reporting and the finished product? That is a question I am often asked. The answer is that it does not. A *Time* reporter's job is to try to place the writer and editor in the most knowledgeable stance possible before a story is written, edited and committed to print. A well reported and a well written *Time* story have very much in common. From Washington, our writers and editors expect the most responsible and expert guidance, and when this is forthcoming the product is based foursquare upon the reporting. The flow of ideas through the entire Time organization is a free one. We *do* seek a consensus of opinion and conviction between reporter and writer and editor, and sometimes we seek to revoke a consensus in the nation. But with it, we cannot evade the demand for a general coherence and for a clear sense of direction. This must come from the Editor-in-Chief, for many years Henry R. Luce, and now Hedley Donovan. It is the Editor-in-Chief who can and must be held broadly accountable for the policies of his publications.

Then, too, the question often is raised with me by journalism students particularly, concerning *Time's "objectivity."* From its very first days, in 1923, *Time* believed that so-called "objectivity" in journalism had become, as practiced, too often a word synonymous with aridity, with journalistic laziness, with ineptitude, with lack of taste and lack of courage. *Time* believed that its function was to go far beyond telling merely what happened. It has been interested, throughout its history, in values, in judgments, in the meaning of the world about us. I suppose the highest master of the art of "objectivity" was an old fellow, now long gone to his Maker, whom I used to watch occasionally as he practiced his profession at the National Press Club bar. His practice was to take copies of government press releases and speeches given in Congress, mark them up with a black grease pencil, changing not a word or a comma, and then telegraph them to his home office. The old boy was lucky: he went to heaven before his paper got wise and sent him somewhere else.

*Time* Inc. always has denied that its function was one of antiseptic objectivity. We never have claimed to be neutral in any fight; we do claim to be fair. Our occasional lapses in this respect, and they are occasional, have hurt us. And our judgments on occasion have been shown to be wrong. But that's part of the risk of the game we play hard and well each week.

## 12

## TELLING THE STORY WITH PHOTOS

### By ARTHUR ROTHSTEIN

The so-called "communications business" began with two Cro-Magnon men, according to the latest scholarly research.

One of these two early "communicators" was fleet of foot and loud of lung. It was this "communicator" who bulletined the community with items like, "Henry has just been eaten by a sabre-tooth."

The other early "communicator" sat around the fire at night and asked, "Why was Henry eaten by the sabre-tooth?" In his search for meaning, he gave chalk talks on the wall of the cave so that future generations might not only see the sabre-tooth at lunch and, by implication, how to avoid him, but also how a society should be structured to avoid the problems posed by this kind of situation.

Photojournalism has evolved from the second of these two "communicators."

The essence of photojournalism is anticipation, believability, significance.

"Anticipation" because our kind of photojournalism does not report the news; it anticipates what an audience will want and need to know.

"Believability" because photographers and writers must live with a story if the audience is to believe the photographs are what they purport to be.

"Significance" because stories without it will soon bore, and we will quickly lose our audience. And, when no one is listening, you are, by definition, failing to communicate.

Certain techniques have been developed at Look to help us tell our stories effectively. Briefly, the techniques are these:

*The Idea.* Ideas are our lifeblood. When you are anticipating news, instead of reporting news, you don't have any crutches. You cannot lean on a scandal in government or on a sudden political crisis abroad to bail you out from a dull issue. You must examine hundreds of ideas weekly in order to be ahead of events. Our Editorial Plans Board must anticipate the scandal in government or the political crisis that will seem sudden to most journalists. Once ideas have been selected, they are assigned to senior editors.

*The Background.* The senior editor in charge begins his investigation, assisted by our library and trained research assistants. After he has digested the research, the senior editor must decide if there is, indeed, a story in the idea and, if there is, what direction the story will probably take.

Note the use of the "probably take". The editors will quickly modify or even discard altogether the original idea if they find, when they get out into the field, that the actual facts are not what research had indicated they would be. There is no pressure to make facts fit the story.

*The Photographer.* After conferring with the managing editor, the senior editor will request to have a photographer assigned to the story. Once assigned, the photographer goes over the research with the senior editor.

At this point, our nomenclature changes. The "senior editor" becomes a writer-editor or a writer-editor-producer. No matter what you call him, he's in charge of "the idea" and the words for the story.

*Location.* We feel that the best, if not the only way, to obtain believability is for the writer-photographer team to go out in the field, to live with their story, to learn to know intimately all of the people who comprise their story. Needless to say, this results in believable stories.

Since travel is expensive and film is much less so, our photographers shoot and shoot and shoot. Many of you have heard complaints about the thousands of photographs we've taken in order to get the five or six we ultimately used.

There are good reasons for this procedure. For one thing, the camera has no eraser. You can't fix up your mistakes. For another thing, since our photographers are not there to make the facts conform to a story idea, they must necessarily photograph everything that may ultimately prove to be pertinent. They can't just settle for five or six pictures that might work with the original story idea. Still a third reason is that photographing the same subject from many different ways and different angles gives greater freedom to the art department when they make the layouts.

*Assembly.* Once the photographer is satisfied and the writer (who is generally present for every picture) feels he has his story, the team returns to New York. The photographs are then developed.

## MAGAZINES 53

Frequently the editors decide how much space to give a story by the quality of the photographs. Once the determination of space has been made, the photographs are then taken by the editor, the same editor who has been out on location, to the art director who will be responsible for making up the layout.

If available, the photographer is also present, and he gets involved with the editor and the art director in the production of the layout. The layout is done before a word of text is is written. After the layout has been made and the photographs actually printed up, dummy type is ordered and a complete page is made up to show what the whole layout is going to look like.

*The Writer.* Now the writer gets down to the typewriter. Headlines, picture captions, text—it's all his now. The captions must add a dimension to that which is observable in the photograph. The writer can't just describe that which is visible to the naked eye. His headlines must fairly, but dramatically summarize and "sell" his article. And, the text must come from his experiences in "living the story."

It's a blood, sweat and tears process. We don't have a rewrite desk. Our "copy" people make suggestions in order to help the writer express a thought more perfectly in his own indvidual terms. They do not write it for him.

And, when he's satisfied that he's told his story, that's it. The story is ready for the printer.

In any discussion such as this it would seem appropriate to discuss the people who produce stories.

First, it should be noted, most of them are on our staff. Most of our photographers have a special kind of background and training that they develop as they work for the magazine, making it possible for them to work much more efficiently and to produce a greater volume of usable material.

There are some photographers whom we hire on a free lance basis, but most of these people are specialists in a given field.

You may recently have seen the unusual pictures that Art Kane made to illustrate "Songs of Freedom." Art Kane is basically an illustrating photographer, not a journalist. He was formerly an art director and only later turned to photography. For portraits, we may hire specialists like Arnold Newman or Philippe Halsman.

A second point to be noted is that many are called, but few are chosen.

There is no magic way to become one of those chosen. They do not come from any single college or university. Indeed, a few of them had not even completed their formal education at the time they went work for us. I am thinking primarily of editor Sam Castan, who was killed in action in Vietnam in 1967. Sam was hired despite his somewhat unorthodox credentials because he had in great measure the personal quality we look for.

Lacking a better word for it, I can only call that personal quality "the spark". Sam had it. He wanted to be a great journalist. He was.

If you're looking for a "career in journalism," I can only tell you this: think about it carefully. If you don't really care about the story, and if getting that story and telling it well isn't the most important thing in your life, you might just be making a mistake.

And, speaking of mistakes, we have made some along the way, but on the whole, I think we've done pretty well in keeping faith with the communications approach of our Cro-Magnon ancestor.

For example, when was the last time you saw a sabre-tooth at lunch? And, have you noticed how the society has been structured to work around the dining habits of the sabre-tooth, while neatly confining him to the gas tank? We can't, of course, take all the credit, but we've done what we could.

# 13

# MAGAZINE WRITING AND PHOTOJOURNALISM

## By GILBERT GROSVENOR

Do thoughts of clipping coupons in a stuffy Wall Street office, or pounding the pavement as a door-to-door salesman really excite you? Wouldn't you rather be paid to poke about the ancient ruins of Angkor Wat, or perhaps to explore Tanzania's teeming Serengeti Plains? Though you may accuse me of "place-dropping," if you were a staff writer or photographer for *National Geographic Magazine*, these names would be as familiar to you as New York City.

Magazine journalism offers a cornucopia of excitement, adventure, prestige, and financial reward; but to pluck such plums, I must hastily add, demands talent, hard work, an insatiable desire to excel, and excruciating patience. For young, inexperienced college graduates to break into major publications can be extremely difficult.

The myth that writers are born with a nose for news and that photographers are blessed with a God-given eye for pictures has frightened hundreds of potentially success journalists into other, more secure, but perhaps less rewarding, endeavors. I contend that if you are bright, industrious, and lucky enough to study under a great editor, you can absorb by osmosis that mysterious talent for scenting a story.

Traditionally, an aspiring writer must cub for small daily newspapers, news services, or house organ publications. Gradually, he builds a portfolio sufficient to impress an editor of a major magazine such as the *Geographic*.

For a talented, enterprising photographer the route from the campus darkroom to an illustration editor's light table may be short-cut if he utilizes his college years to assemble photographic portfolios, notably by working with a local daily paper or school news publication.

An affinity for strenuous physical activity should be included among a photographer's credentials. His work day must include the finest light from dawn to midmorning, as well as those final hours before dusk. A twelve-hour day, seven days a week, is not uncommon for a photographer working on a field assignment.

Perhaps the most sought after, but naturally the rarest journalist is the writer-photographer. I can count on the fingers of both hands the ones in this country capable of producing publishable pictures and text for the *Geographic*. This breed must be ambidextrous—taking pictures and recording notes simultaneously. For editors expect the writer-photographer to produce complete coverage within the same time limits allowed for a photographer to shoot the story.

How do you determine whether or not you possess latent journalistic talent? Try it.

As an example of how you might begin, I vividly recall the eager young Dartmouth students who knocked on the editor's door at the *Geographic* five years ago. They outlined in detail summer plans to canoe down the Danube River. Would we be interested? Yes, the trip interested us, but were those students competent journalists? Of course not, but they were willing to learn. Two members of the team mastered the use of long and wide-angle lenses, flash equipment, and different types of color film.

We coached some of them about writing for the *Geographic*, stressed our style, and badgered them to record copious notes, including not only facts but quotes, impressions, descriptions, and moods that make the reader feel he's sharing the experience.

These young men were intelligent; they learned fast. But most significant, they were highly motivated to succeed. The results? In the July, 1965, *National Geographic* we published forty-six pages of text and color photographs on the Danube canoe trip—an excellent coverage. This group was paid more money for a summer vacation than most graduates command their first year out of school. More important, at least one of them now plans to make journalism his profession.

And what is expected of a *Geographic* staffer? Plenty. He must be ready to travel anywhere in the world at a moment's notice. When the Alaska earthquake nudged the seismograph off the Richter scale, our photographer was airborne for Anchorage within a few hours. Only by generously tipping a taxi driver to drive onto the Washington airfield and stop the plane was he able to get aboard. On occasion a staff man will swelter in searing 120°F. heat in Yemen or shiver in numbing –102°F. deep freeze at the South Pole. He may be assigned to dive into the depths of the Red Sea or fly into the stratosphere aboard an experimental aircraft. One staffer, Barry C. Bishop, climbed to the summit of Mount Everest. His remarkable pictures from the roof of the world won international acclaim. Although frostbite cost him his ten toes, it in no way dented his enthusiasm.

*Geographic* writers and photographers frequently assume total editorial responsibility for assignments. For example, Thomas J. Abercrombie was summoned to the editor's office one day last year. "Tom, I want you to cover Saudi Arabia. You make the contacts and arrangements. Visit Mecca if at all possible."

Respecting Tom's ability, the editor offered no further instruction. Weeks of research lay ahead. Scores of introductory letters would have to be written, and conferences with embassy contacts arranged, before Abercrombie could intelligently undertake a major assignment in such a seldom-traveled area. Enrolling in night school classes, he boned up on Arabic, which he had taught himself on a previous assignment in Yemen and still practiced at home in case he again drew an assignment to an Arab-speaking nation. He also had become a Moslem.

Traveling 20,000 miles by jet, automobile, donkey and camel, Tom criss-crossed Saudi Arabia from Jidda to Riyadh. To absorb the flavor of this fascinating country, he hitched rides with camel caravans, learning to steer by the stars across the trackless sands. By Land-Rover he probed deep into the Empty Quarter, where even the Saudis fear to travel, in search of a rumored meteorite. Incredibly, he found it. Climaxing his assignment, Tom joined fellow Moslems for the annual pilgrimage to Mecca, where he was admitted to the brotherhood of Islam. Never before had Saudi Arabia been so beautifully photographed, agreed both the *Geographic's* editor and Arabia's King Faisal Saud.

The one attribute which binds all journalists togther—whether cub reporters or Nobel Prize-winners—can best be defined as "hunger." This hunger if whetted by the lure of the quest, the drive for recognition, the insatiable desire to tell a story in words or pictures, and to a lesser extent the financial reward. But once the hunger is satisfied a journalist is finished. Never have I seen a complacent writer or photographer produce a top-notch story.

Only you can determine whether you are hungry enough to put your potential to the test. But be assured that should you choose journalism as a profession you will lead a stimulating life filled with rewarding experiences throughout the world.

## 14

## WORDS WILL ALWAYS COUNT

*By* Arnold Gingrich

With your indulgence, I should like to amplify the title of a talk I gave at a recent meeting of the Magazine Publishers Association. For the record, "Words Will Always Count" will suffice. But for the actual presentation, the full title is needed. And mine is: *Words Will Always Count, and Computers are Marvelous but They Kiss Not, Neither Do They Cook, and Besides, McLuhanism is Only One Part Logic and Three Parts Pie-in-the-Eye.*

For all the razzle dazzle of electronic marvels both here and to come, Euclid has yet to be eclipsed, and Molière, while succeeded by McLuhan, has not been supplanted. In short, a straight line is still the shortest distance between two points, no matter how fancifully you may bad-mouth the Linear Age that was ushered in by the invention of movable type, and there are still some things of which it may be said that the more they change the more they are the same.

The other day a skywriter in a plane went up over Long Island and, in letters that looked a mile high, spelled out *Happy Birthday Abe.* Well, it cost four hundred dollars, and I guess you'd have to concede that this was a pretty clear cut case where "the medium is the message," but the words were no different than if Abe's wife had simply baked a cake.

The logistics and the technique and the medium were certainly different, but the message was the same. While a skywriter is by now a quaint and corny and old-fashioned thing, even the newest of the most sophisticated phase of computers couldn't have said it any better.

You can get a computer to say "I love you," but you can't program it into saying it with feeling, and meaning it and, saddest lack of all, doing anything about it. But I cheerfully concede that you can get it to do almost anything else that you or I can do.

As E. B. Weiss pointed out in his series of articles in *Advertising Age* on the communications revolution, until the advent of the computer, modern society seemed in danger of drowning in a sea of white paper.

I am reminded of what Field Marshal Mongtomery said when a reporter asked him in the spring of '45 if the war would end soon. He said it would have to, or all the armies everywhere would run out of paper. This is one thing that, thanks to the new computer-connected banks of data storage, we don't have to fear in the future.

Through instant retrieval, on demand, of stored materials on microfilm and videotape (a single reel of which can store a half million pages of documents) computer printouts can now make things available with incredible speed, whether they are published, unpublished or long out of print. Already, according to the Weiss series, computers print out more original material in a month than all of the nation's book publishers do in years.

This form of "on demand" printing, or as I think of it, of custom publishing, has indeed brought the age of Gutenberg full circle, and have by a magnificent irony progressed right back to where we were in the fourteenth century, in the age of the monasteries, when movable type didn't matter because it didn't exist. We can now have a copy—an edition of one, on demand—of almost anything almost anywhere. The difference is that today it is done by a machine working minutes to hours, whereas then it was done laboriously and painstakingly by a monk working months to years.

Willy nilly, one must agree with McLuhan on this; what price movable type, when anything, anywhere, that has been written or diagrammed or drawn can now be facsimile-produced on demand for as few or as many as may want it? As Weiss pointed out, this aspect of publishing has proceeded circularly, from the handwritten manuscript book, to the limited editions of the earliest printing presses, to the mammoth editions of the latest printing presses, and now, back again, to the single copy produced on demand.

It may be unfair to oversimplify McLuhanism into the bare statement that our Visual Age, bred of reading linear type, has been superseded by an Audio Age, in which we are conditioned rather by the multi-directional impulses of electronic sound. But since this is certainly a recognizable part of the famous "message that is the medium that is the message," it may be fair to take issue with it on the ground that it can equally well be argued that we are still in a fairly early stage of the visual revolution that began with the Gutenberg Press and Renaissance Art.

The visual perception of Americans in the mass has only recently begun to flourish on any meaningful scale. There is a quickening visual awareness that is at least seeping, if not actually sweeping, across the country that embraces beauty of design in all things: from op art mini dresses to sculptured kitchen gadgets to exotic objects of art to exquisitely tuned motorcars to resplendent cultural centers. These are all aspects of the Visual Age; it would seem that its impact is only beginning to be felt.

In other words, the great leveling upward of incomes that has characterized this nation since the end of World War II has been paralleled by a similar leveling upward of standards of taste and appreciation, and education and sophistication, with the result that great numbers of Americans are only beginning to say Hello to the phenomena of our Visual Age, to which the impetuous professor can't wait to say Goodbye.

It may not have been McLuhan himself who first made the statement that I have often heard echoed in discussions of his theories, that "books will be museum pieces in a decade."

But with the possibilities of mass copying being opened up by inventions like IBM's photo-image retrieval system, which can store five hundred thousand microfilm images and produce a copy of any one in several seconds, I think it can be argued just as logically that a lot of things that are now *only* museum pieces will in another decade enjoy the same widespread and casual public currency that is now afforded only by books.

Certainly, since the paperback revolution, we have seen many books that were only "museum pieces" a mere decade or so ago find the wide currency of availability on any corner newsstand or drugstore.

We all tend, from time to time, to confuse the medium with the message; and we do it every time there is a new medium. I'm old enough to remember the beginning of radio, and how it led a lot of people to throw out their phonographs on the assumption that the new invention had superannuated the old. And in the early days of TV there were frequent references by comedians to radio, always followed by the stock crack, "if you remember what that is." So Professor McLuhan, in vaunting the new at the expense of the old, is only giving an old joke a new twist.

And speaking of new twists, there's the story of the computer that was asked if there is a God, and answered instantly, "There is now."

With the third generation of computers, we have had a spate of speculation over the possibility of making "machines that think." I don't know why this should be so speculative. Of course these machines can think. Within a certain range of thought processes, where the simultaneous consideration of a broad and complex range of variables is involved, machines can outthink even the most gifted of humans. For analytical and evaluative processes of a bewilderingly complex nature, where the multiplicity of factors would tax human memory and application to an intolerable degree, the machine is beyond question's man's superior, and should and will be used more and more for these reckonings for which the human mind is too slow, too uneconomical to be employed for such extensive drudgery.

For just one prosaic example, anybody who has ever compiled an index will cheerfully concede that this is one thinking job that only a machine is really fit for.

At this early phase of the space age, it is already possible to cite a number of instances where the computer has already outthought man, both as to the speed and the complexity of the thought process. So it is probably safe to say that the machine can think as well or better than a man can, over the entire range of *tactical* thinking—the situations where prior knowledge of past problems solved, infallibly retrieved and applied, is sufficient. Where the machine can't go is only where very few exceptional humans can go successfully—into the upper reaches of thought, the level of *strategic* thinking, where hunch, insight, intuition, or inspired guesswork can make the difference between winning and losing, between invention and disruption, between creation and destruction—in other words, into the rarefied strata of *creative* thinking.

The computer, in short, can think of nothing that hasn't been thought of before, which is the best reason I can adduce as to why computers will never replace editors. The machine is limited to facts —it can never muddle or stumble its way beyond and above the sum total to reach the blinding revelation of the truth.

On the other hand, computers do enjoy certain advantages over humans, other than greater speed and competency that it would be unfair not to point out. True, they can neither kiss nor cook, but neither can they pout. Tell a computer to forget something, and it will be forgotten as completely as if it never occurred or existed. I can think of no editors, living or dead, of whom that could be said.

Yes, these machines are clever, and they do present us many a dilemma. The old time politician's answer to a dilemma has gone into the language as the colloquialism "if you can't lick 'em, join 'em," and that may well be the best answer. Peaceful coexistence with the machines may best be assured by coalition, or by merger, between the mechanical and the human elements in publishing, between the tactical and the strategic, the clerical and the creative.

In the realm of book publishing, this is already the name of the game. With mergers accomplished, pending, imminent and rampant, the book publishing scene today resembles a game of musical chairs. And so far as I can distinguish from a seat in the outfield bleachers, all the sounds emanating from that melee so far are happy ones, with everybody apparently winning all around.

I will cite just one example, of a segment of the book publishing scene with which I have had a thirty-three years firsthand acquaintance.

Alfred A. Knopf has for over fifty years been known as one of the most fastidious, and most ruggedly, almost fiercely individualistic, of all American book publishers. There's nobody I can think of less likely to be caught keeping company with a computer. But some years ago, Alfred A. Knopf, Inc. was merged with a larger publishing concern, Random House, and subsequently, Random House itself was merged with RCA. Does this sound like the path to oblivion for the corporate identity of the party of the first part? Well, in some businesses it might, but in the book business it doesn't seem to work out that way. Knopf books, over the years and through two mergers, have lost not one iota of their uniquely distinctive identity and not one whit of their long known and respected editorial integrity. What *has* happened is that the sales and production and distribution facilities of a smaller publisher have been greatly improved, through enjoying the advantages implicit in merging these non-creative aspects of the business—which in no way affect the nature of the product—with those of a larger concern, effecting economies and efficiencies that would not otherwise be available to the smaller and more individual firm.

This is, as I say, just one example of the intelligent use of improved and enhanced mechanical facilities without detriment to the product itself. This is a case of enlightened mastery of the machine, with no apparent danger of ever becoming its slave. It may have some value as an example of how the creative can happily cohabit with the mechanical.

Since our very product is intelligence, it behooves us to be eternally vigilant lest we allow it to become adulterated by unintelligent handling or practice. Asking a computer to do any but the routine and mechanical and "housekeeping" aspects of an editor's job would not be a very intelligent thing to do, at least for those aspects of the editorial content of a magazine that rise above the level of mere listings; expecting a computer to edit would be like asking the students to take over the teaching, the unions to take over the management, the robbers to take over the police force, the—well, the mind boggles at the mounting enormity of these analogies, but I can still think of a worse one—it's like asking the *readers* to take over the editing.

Asking a reader what he would like to see in a magazine is only a means of finding out what he *has* liked. And that's all a computer can tell you, for all its dazzling and superhuman ability to reel off at instant notice everything it's been programmed into learning by rote.

As someone said the other day, "the printed word was first." This is another way of reminding us of the fundamental truth—I'm almost tempted to say the fundamentalistic truth—"in the beginning was the Word."

It was the word that first distinguished us from the animals in our long upward climb from the ooze and slime of our primordial beginning; and it is the word that will always distinguish us, no matter what new tricks we teach them, from the machines.

It was the words that, when Shakespeare's tongue had long ago turned to dust, made good his promise that they would outlive many a prince's guilded monument.

We can build bigger and better, we can go farther and faster; but we can't catch up with Tintoretto or with Turner in the likeness of a sunset, nor match the blue of a Veronese sky, nor isolate, with all our scientific skills, the golden gleam of the varnish on a Stradivarius, nor can we turn a sonnet with the skill of Keats or Shelley or Milton.

In a creative business, such as ours, the quantitative factors are subject to infinite enhancement, through electronic and mechanical miracles now present and still to come, but the qualitative elements, thank God, are still subject to improvement only through such old-fashioned means as elbow grease and midnight oil. And let's be glad of it, for otherwise we could all be replaced, and there'd be nobody left to come here each year, and enjoy the beauties of a place like this.

## 15

## THE ART OF EDITING

### By ROBERT STEIN

Walter Slezak, the actor, once told a story about prompters in the theatre. "Nobody," he said, "sets out to be a prompter. No parent looks at a child in the cradle and says, 'that boy is going to be a great prompter some day'. It just happens." The same, at least until recently, has been true about magazine editors.

Magazine editing is largely an accidental profession, drifted into by happenstance or circumstance, usually through newspapering. I know; I have gone that way myself, although I did discover magazines when I was in my last year at college. A friend had uncovered the fact that you could write articles for magazines without being on the staff, and even get paid for them. Together, we started to collaborate, and that was how I was first exposed to magazines.

Today, as chairman of the American Society of Magazine Editors, I am involved in a program that hopefully will attract young people to magazine careers, and help them learn about the field while they are still in college. Such an internship program for juniors and seniors will, we hope, be instituted within the year. And it is high time, too. Magazine editing, on all levels, is a career with a future.

Magazine people have gotten over their initial fear that television is a monster that will destroy them, just as newspaper people recovered from their fear of radio, and earlier, magazines got over their dread of radio and the movies. Each medium that comes along doesn't destroy all other media; it simply changes the range of possibilities. And television has, if anything, opened new horizons for magazines. By taking over the job of providing light entertainment for millions, it has left magazines free to concentrate on more substantial levels of information and entertainment.

How do you edit a magazine? All good editors I know start with their own convictions and interests and as much imagination as they can within the framework of what their magazine is trying to accomplish. Sometimes they cannot do things they believe are worthwhile because their judgment tells them they can't find a way of reaching enough readers with a particular idea.

But they are constantly trying to find ways to translate things that are important to them, as citizens and as human beings, into terms that are effective and meaningful to their readers. That is why magazine editing is such an exciting job. That is why it should be attracting young people today.

What I would tell the young writer today who wants to work for a magazine? For one, I would not put too much emphasis on preparation in terms of specific skills. I think these skills are sharpened with experience, though I do think it is valuable to learn the techniques of writing, research and interviewing.

What is more important for the young writer, banal as it may sound, is to develop himself as a person, and to explore and expand his own range of interests. It is this awareness of himself and his possibilities that will lead him toward what he can do best.

I've seen some very good writers develop in magazines—and the best were those who followed their own instincts and their own interests, who did not tailor-make their work for what they thought were the requirements of editors. They sometimes suffered a material loss—at least at the beginning, before they were recognized—but they always turned out to be not only more effective, but also more successful in the commercial sense.

I am not saying that it is always possible to take what you're most interested in and excited about, and use it directly in the largest magazines. But if you do take the material closest to you, and try to find suitable publications, including small magazines with small budgets, they will give you the opportunity to develop. Prefabricating for a given market, imitating a formula, is always dangerous.

Markets and formulas change, and so do editors, and what matters in the long run is your own integrity and talent.

One of the rewards for all the work magazine editors do, all the frustrations we encounter, all the distress we endure, is the feeling that magazines are particularly suited for helping to keep people human in a society where it is increasingly difficult to stay human.

When I, or any other editor of a large magazine, see millions of magazines stacked in one place at the printing plant, it's an awesome sight. But what I, and other editors, work from is a sense of talking to one individual at a time, in a way that will be most effective and useful, whether the subject is religion, recipes or student rebellion. Sometimes they are failures. But even failures are debatable. An article may not have meant much to a majority of readers, yet it may have touched some lives in an important way.

## 16

## SPORTSWRITING

*By* AL SILVERMAN

One of the first stories I was asked to edit early in my career was by John Lardner on prize fighter Stanley Ketchel. Lardner's third paragraph started like this:
"There's a story by Ernest Hemingway, 'The Light of the World,' in which a couple of boys on the road sit listening to a pair of seedy harlots as they trade lies about how they loved the late Stanley Ketchel in person. This is the mythology of the hustler—the shiniest lie the girls can manage, the invocation of the top name in the folklore of sporting life."

For some reason, I have always remembered that passage of Lardner's. (By the way, I should clear up what I mean when I said I was asked to *edit* Lardner. Being a novice with the magazine, the editor gave me the Lardner story with the explicit advice not to touch anything. "Just put the paragraph marks in," he said. He was right of course. Lardner worked very hard on his writing—three, four, five drafts—and like any good writer, took editing badly.)

To this day, the memory of John Lardner's writing sustains me, especially when I have to deal with those writers who are uncomfortable in the presence of the English language.

It was Roger Kahn, another admirable writer on sports, who made the observation that "sportswriting was not the craft of John Lardner . . . his craft was purely writing: writing the English sentence, fusing sound and meaning, matching the precision of the word with the rhythm of the phrase." Kahn was right about that but wrong to say that sportswriting was not John Lardner's craft. Sure it was, and why be defensive about it?

The trouble is that all of us who work around the fringe of sports—as paid observers—tend to be faintly defensive about our livelihood. I think perhaps that is really why I remember so vividly that segment from Lardner's Ketchel story—because he used a literary reference to set up the significance of Ketchel as a sports figure.

I somehow found that comforting; that sports and literature could be so intertwined.

# MAGAZINES

When I came out of college with a journalism degree, I had vague ideas about going to work for the *Boston Globe* or the *New York Times,* and writing about cosmic subjects. In those days I was regularly submitting bad short stories of a cosmic nature to the *Partisan Review* and *Commentary.* My cosmic period ended suddenly when I was thrust onto a sport magazine. At the time I looked upon it as a bad piece of casting but, hell, it was the best editorial job I could find in New York City, and it saved me from returning, empty, to the provinces.

I was able to console myself by invoking, like Lardner's hustlers, the names of those who had dwelt on sports at one time or other in their careers—Hemingway, London, Turqenev, Fitzgerald, Faulkner, Mann.

The trouble was in my psyche, of course. As a boy I had loved sports. I had loved to play sports and I had loved to root for teams. I followed the Boston Braves, for instance, with the hopeless passion of a Cyrano.

But never in my most rococo dreams did it occur to me that I might someday make a living from sports. My father, after all, was a tailor. He had never had time to play at sports, let alone earn money from sports (except on those infrequent occasions when he scored a "hit" on the numbers or at the racetrack). Now I was working for a sport magazine, doing something that had consumed me as a boy. Was this the fulfillment of the American dream? I was embarrassed.

I am no more. I recall now that I loved good writing as a boy, too, and when I found out that sportswriting and good writing could be quite compatible, my mortification soon washed away.

This is true, of course. I discovered "the truth" first from John Lardner, and it was reinforced as I read over manuscripts written by W. C. Heinz, Roger Kahn, Ed Linn, Myron Cope, Arnold Hano, Jimmy Breslin, Dick Schaap.

And I am constantly renewed when a new young writer, a *real* writer, is unearthed, when he delivers a manuscript that bursts with clarity, imagination, originality—style.

Sophisticated sportswriting in the best Lardner tradition is the trend these days, and I am thankful that it is. Paul Gallico, a reformed sportswriter, once referred to the sportswriters of the 1920's as the "Gee-whizzers." They were the suckers, he said, "for the theology of the good guys and the bad guys."

Gee-whiz, no more.

Today, the good writer will back off and take a hard look at the athlete or the event in all his or its dimensions—black, white, grey and shades of grey. The good writer has been doing this for some time in the magazines, and now, thankfully, the trend has spread to the newspapers.

There is on our land today, particularly in the New York area, a breed of newspaper sportswriters who typify the new left in sportswriting. They are known as "the chipmunks" (a nickname of uncertain derivation). The specialty of the chipmunks is to probe for the human qualities in the athlete. The chipmunks always ask the tough question—"how did you feel when?"—even when failure, not success, is involved. The most famous chipmunk-type question came the day the New York Yankees were celebrating a 1962 World Series victory over the San Francisco Giants. The winning pitcher was Ralph Terry and his wife had just called to congratulate him and tell hm that their new baby was coming along fine.

"What's you wife doing?" a reporter asked.

"Feeding the baby," said Terry.

A chipmunk was ready. "Breast or bottle?" he asked.

It is symptomatic of the new atmosphere in sports that Ralph Terry answered that question. The growing sophistication of the athlete himself has helped considerably. It is so difficult to write a lively magazine profile on a lumpen of an athlete; and twenty years ago the lumpens owned the sports world. No more. Today, more athletes have college educations, more athletes have better minds, more athletes have worldly outlooks, more athletes are unafraid to reveal to the public the subtleties and complexities of their nature.

In almost every issue we put together, we find at least one fullbodied subject to throw alongside the inevitable clod. Don Meredith, once a quarterback for the Dallas Cowboys, is an example. Meredith was sometimes considered a lackadaisical football player. "That was just my way," he said. "I can't wear a long face and be somber. But some players didn't understand this. They thought I was carefree, unconcerned (and you know my heart was breaking under this clown's costume) . . . I'm naturally gregarious, but I had to pull away from the team as individuals. I had to become a loner. Yes, ensign, it's a lonely life here on the bridge."

Life has become much less lonely, ensigns, writing about such free spirits as Meredith. And much, much less lonely writing about them for magazines. For this is a far more expressive medium than daily newspapers, and it constantly bugs me that more young people do not seek careers as writers and editors on magazines. Lord knows, we need them. Yet those who are motivated towards journalism still head for the daily newspaper, and ignore the magazine.

It is, when all is said and done, good work writing for magazines and editing magazines. Every month there is the creation again, a brand new universe. And if that universe feeds off sports, what of it? Sports, surely, is an integral part of our culture. I do not ascribe any mystical reasons why this should be so. Maybe sports at its basic level does reinforce man's masculinity, as the pop psychologists say.

We know that sports is a prime subject of mentalk, rivalled only by topics of seduction and money. We know too that sports is essentially frivolous in nature—"fun and games, not life and death," as one of the chipmunks put it. But sports is also, for better or worse, a reflection of our true selves. I leave it to Ed Linn, the Santayana of the profession, for the last word: "The marvelous part of sports is that somebody wins and somebody loses, while in your own life it is sometimes hard to tell whether you've won or lost or, indeed, whether you've been in the game."

## 17

## APPRAISING FICTION

### By ROBERT BROWN

There is so little fiction published by magazines that can afford to pay their editors that it is foolish to think of being a "fiction editor" as a career.

Off-hand, I can think only of *Esquire, The New Yorker* and *Playboy*. I don't think any other magazine hires anyone to deal only with fiction.

How does one get these jobs? I don't know. I got mine because I met the then fiction editor of *Esquire* in a poker game. We became friends; a couple of years later he was in the market for a first-reader and I was it.

Of course he knew by then that I had a more or less appropriate background: had been in graduate school, taught, etc. Were—are—these academic credentials relevant? In the long run I suppose the answer must be "yes."

What a fiction editor does, at *Esquire,* is "process" an endless stream of manuscripts, more than he can possibly read. He buys or, in 99 cases out of 100, rejects.

What he must be able to do is make very fast and very accurate rejections, sending back most stuff unfinished. "What, Sir, do you read books through?" (The longer one is out of school the less confident will be his allusions to Dr. Johnson.)

Anything he considers buying is, of course, read carefully and then passed on to his superiors. With these he may argue if the mood is on him or the piece in question is of unusual interest. In most cases there is fairly close agreement or, if not, the story may be marginal anyway and not worth making a fight about. In my five years at *Esquire,* I can remember only two or three cases where my best efforts were not enough to prevent a major error.

But I was talking about the academic background. In order to be able to reject—with confidence—work that you have not finished reading, it is necessary to convince yourself that years of studying literature at the highest level have so refined the palate, so imbued you with an intuitive understanding of the way it all works, that

# MAGAZINES

judgment does its work with a precision and speed the conscious mind cannot articulate. Like a pianist's fingers. One does not need to explain to each author or agent just why his story failed to please.

It is good practise to be encouraging sometimes, even though you haven't bought the story; you may want the author to send more. In general, a fiction editor should try to keep himself informed about who is doing what and whether or not he can see it: One does that by reading a lot and occasionally having lunch with agents.

Manuscripts come in sponsored by agents or unsolicited, and it is customary to have a reader weed out obvious lunatics from the unsolicited pile and pass on only the best of the rational work. In theory, the agents have done that before sending *their* things out; in practise, it is sometimes the case.

But the New York literary world, in its commercial aspect, is not distinguished by a large number of finely developed sensibilities. We're all in it for a buck, you understand, and presumably many agents feel that there is nothing to lose by sending a story along. What the hell, someone may buy it.

There is nothing reprehensible in this, any more than there is in a publisher accepting a book he knows will sell like mad even though it's pretty lousy. But perhaps this is all too obvious to need explaining.

On a general magazine there is frequently welcome relief to be had in working on projects that have nothing to do with fiction.

I myself found considerable satisfaction in selecting the girls for a calendar in the Christmas issue of 1965 and getting them photographed; I never got more than six months finished and had to invent some gibberish to explain to our readers why we were presenting a calendar for only half a year. That done, it was back to the Jewish novelists and short story writers.

## 18

## SPECIALIZED PUBLICATIONS

### By JOHN B. BABCOCK

Would you believe *Fertility and Sterility? Macaroni Journal? Mortuary Management? Corset & Underwear Review? Reproduction Review?*

Yes, Virginia, there are such publications in America. And hundreds more with equally strange sounding names—ranging from *Corrosion* to *Journal of Symbolic Logic*. . . . from *Refuse Removal Journal* and *Pest Control* to *Who's Who in the Hatchery World* and *Homiletic and Pastoral Review*.

While they may not be the names that customarily send visions of Pulitzer Prizes dancing in the heads of aspiring journalists, they and their 2,600 fellow specialized business publications are very important to the future well-being of America.

They generate the necessary exchange of information and ideas to keep our complex economy moving forward. Whatever the format—magazine, newspaper, or directory—and whether publication is on a daily, weekly, or monthly basis, the business press penetrates every corner of the economy . . . distributing, interpreting, and analyzing specialized know-how as fast as it emerges.

Accordingly, the business press offers jobs that are challenging, exciting and rewarding for the fellow or girl who likes to find out the facts and their significance, and write about them impartially, accurately, and lucidly for an informed and influential audience.

Informed and influential it is. The business press readership numbers 62 million, including the nation's leaders in well over 150 different businesses and professions that affect the lives of us all. The fact that this readership bases many of its key decisions on what's printed in the business publications it has come to respect is one of the substantial plus factors of employment by these journals.

Another plus: business press editorial people—about 14,000 of the 70,000 men and women employed—are *doers,* whether they are reporting on the retail business or flying into the Canadian wilderness to talk to miners.

In Vietnam, you'll find some of the correspondents assigned to cover the war have business press credentials. These newsmen represent publications that cover not only obvious fields of specialization relating to the conflict, such as aviation, medicine, government, and construction, but also such areas as packaging, textiles, and apparel.

Away from war, business reporters and editors are also on the go—attending trade shows, crawling into turbines, making their way across skyscraper scaffolding, sloshing in newly-dug tunnels—involving themselves to get stories and gain greater understanding of the fields they cover.

You'll find great integrity in business journalism. Editors call-them-as-they-see-'em; some are crusaders. They can hardly afford to be otherwise if they want to earn and keep the respect of such sophisticated and knowledgeable readership.

One trade editor learned that a major company was about to introduce a revolutionary product that would render its current output obsolete. When he went to the company for comment, the manufacturer urged him to "sit" on the story because it would hurt current business. When he refused, the manufacturer threatened to withdraw his considerable advertising from the editor's publication. The story ran, and the company did pull its advertising.

But the publication had done its job and intensified its reputation for being on top or ahead of the news. Six months later, the advertiser returned, but even if he hadn't, the publication would have been content—one more illustration of a business publication's willingness to sacrifice revenue to preserve its editorial integrity.

The business press has many virtues, one of the most important of which is impact. The specialized business publications have improved standards in their industries; they've sped the dissemination of scientific knowledge, thereby accelerating progress and new discoveries; they've stimulated the development of new and more efficient business methods; and they've encouraged self-regulation of business.

A business publication reporter has unlimited opportunity to influence change. For example:

• A business publication in the hospital field accused hospitals of being unsanitary and described the problems and causes of hospital-acquired infections. Ways to combat the danger were discussed, and many hospitals used the suggestions as a basis for remedial action.

• A business publication in the trucking industry, in an issue called "Drugs—the Deadly Highway Menace," called attention to the dangers of stay-awake pep pills taken by truck drivers. A focal point of Congressional hearings, the article helped bring about legislation and ICC regulations prohibiting truck drivers from carrying drugs in their vehicles.

Risking electrocution an editor for an electrical publication dramatically demonstrated (in a wire bathtub) the hazards of high voltage wiring in lighted swimming pools. Ultimately, the publication was able to convince electrical manufacturers to produce harmless 12-volt fixtures, and the rate of lethal electric shocks in home pools dropped from an average of one a month to zero.

There are many other such examples, but I think these make the point: What a business publication editor both writes and does has impact.

Of course, scoops and exposes and crusades don't come every day or in every issue. But there's excitement even in the every-day coverage. If you had the chance to study business publications as I have, you'd feel the sense of aliveness that exists in the business press. For hidden there is the greatest crystal ball any fortune teller ever possessed. The editorial pages of the business press contain the headlines of tomorrow.

Before you read about it in the consumer press, business publications were telling readers—in depth—about such futuristic matters as completely automated plants run by button-pushers, and a machine that, in one operation, will dig, lay and finish a continuous ribbon of highway, even coating it with a chemical to make it skidproof.

In an age of specialization, it's the business reporter or editor who is the prime specialist. He's got to know his field—and know it expertly. This is a lot more demanding, but also ultimately more rewarding, than the lack of expertise that necessarily saddles the general reporter on a daily paper, who (according to the textbook) has to be prepared to cover murder in the morning, a Boy Scout meeting in the afternoon, and a fire or political speech at night.

He can hardly hope to be an expert in all these areas, but the business publication editor has to be in his.

Many a business publication is admiringly (and often deservedly) referred to by its readers as the industry's "bible," and those who produce that "bible" are often regarded as prophets. It's frequently a very personal sort of journalism, which doesn't mean the trade newsman is any less objective than his confrere on the consumer daily, but, rather, that he gets to be especially well known and respected in his field.

# MAGAZINES

Admittedly, the fellow who embarks on a career in business journalism has to be willing to adopt a sort of editorial tunnel vision. He has to always interpret what's happening in terms of what it means to the men in the industry he's reporting. Actually, it isn't much different in spirit, however, from the editor of the Main Street Bugle who gives prominence to—and seeks out—the Main Street angle in any news event.

Not only must the good business newsman appreciate and understand his field; not only must he be objective and enterprising. He must be able to write on even complex technical matters with clarity. The story that says it in a lively, imaginative way, without sacrificing accuracy or yielding to sensationalism for its own sake, is especially prized. The decision makers who read the business press are busy men, besieged by reading matter. For them, the motto "time is money" has real application.

As you may have guessed, the pay varies widely, according to the publication and its profit-making potential, as well as the abilities of the staffers. There are business publication editors making $9,000 a year . . . and $29,000 a year. The good business publication will compete with all other media for the top talent that makes a publication good. Starting salaries are competitive with—and in a number of cases higher than—those in consumer media. Some recent median figures (the middle 50 percent) show beginners in all phases of business publishing making between $4,000 and $6,000 a year; editors-in-chief, $10,000 to $20,000; other editors, $6,500 to $15,000.

There are, of course, other worthwhile careers available in business publishing which also require sharp, skilled, intellectually curious and honest people. Many of these are in advertising and circulation, which, with editorial, comprise what some refer to as the three-legged stool of business publications.

In terms of working conditions, fields covered, quality of coverage, and determination to do an honest, meaningful journalistic job, the business press has come a long way since it originated in the 15th century with that distinguished journal, "News Tidings of the House of Fugger." But, as complex as the business world has become, the requirements are fundamentally the same: we still need *special* people for a very *special* kind of work.

If you qualify and if you'd like to tackle a challenge as exciting as tomorrow, by all means look for a job with the business press.

## 19

## WRITING ABOUT BUSINESS

*By* JAMES W. MICHAELS

I don't believe there is such a thing as "business journalism". Those of us associated with magazines about business are simply practicing journalism, period. Business happens to be our beat.

One of our brightest writers puts it like this: "I don't buy the term business journalism anymore than I would buy athletic journalism. Dammit, these are just the beats, the particular facet of life you are covering."

Lincoln Steffens would have approved of what the writer is saying. In Steffens' *Autobiography,* the famed muckraker describes the years he spent covering Wall Street and business. They taught him that there is no such thing as "business" reporting or "political" reporting but that the two are intimately intertwined and require the same skills.

When I say "business" reporting, I do not mean trade journalism. It is far removed from the old fashioned "six-ways-to-improve-your-sales" kind of business magazine. It starts where conventional business reporting leaves off.

The best business writing is about people doing things.

A very intelligent corporate vice president once told me that he regards the top business magazines as drama critics for the business community. "You come out of a story saying that so-and-so is smart and is putting on a fine corporate performance; while so-and-so is dull and a flop."

You can say it another way. A good reporter helps keep politicians on their toes. We try to help keep businessmen and businesses on their toes. This is what good business reporting does: it makes judgments, distributes praise and blame. The business community needs this kind of interpretive reporting.

If a businessman goes bankrupt or goes to Brazil he makes the newspapers and news magazines. But who criticizes him if he constantly misses opportunities and merely drifts along on the momentum and capital that his predecessors have stored up? That's a job of fact-gathering and fact-interpreting that only business magazines have the staff, the know-how and the space to do.

This isn't muckraking, mind you. We simply happen to feel that incompetent management is more of a menace to the free enterprise system than all the socialists and anarchists you can find.

We're equally interested, of course, in the businessman who is doing a really good job, who is overcoming obstacles, who has new ideas. But we're not content with merely putting this fellow on a pedestal. We don't just want to tell *what* he did, but *how* he did it—and *why*.

The best writers for this kind of editorial product are not to be had from the regular business or trade press. Rather they are people, mostly young people, with a liberal arts background, who look at businesses and businessmen as part of the real world, not as abstractions.

Our staff is a good example. One of our senior editors is a former college teacher of English. Another is a former national affairs editor of *Newsweek*. Our Washington bureau manager is a former foreign correspondent (in Latin America).

I didn't even go into "business" journalism until I was in my mid-thirties, and I spent many years as a correspondent in India for United Press International.

One of the best "business" writers ever to come our way was a New York City schoolteacher who later became a sports writer for a national news magazine and drifted into corporate public relations. We rescued him on the reasoning that if he could apply all that experience to our subject, he couldn't miss. He didn't miss.

Wide-awake, iconoclastic, question-asking people are worth the chance. We want individualists who are interested in the whole world around them. If these individualists happen to be M.B.A.'s so much the better, because they already have a basic background in business.

Nearly every year we hire several M.B.A.'s from leading universities, but we don't hire them simply for their degrees. We want M.B.A's who combine an ability to express themselves with a real desire to learn how business really operates.

All this is reflected in the wide range of positions which recent alumni have attained. One is assistant editor of a famous liberal magazine. Yet another, Dick Kluger, after starting *Book Week Magazine*, is now managing editor at Simon & Schuster.

For the big money, our editorial alumni include two partners of Wall Street houses, the marketing vice president of the American

Tobacco Company, and the young founder of a TV sales organization.

As you can see, the business beat is not a dead-end beat. To attract young men of this caliber and of this potential, the best business magazines try to make life interesting and stimulating for their writers. So that the writers remain broadminded rather than become specialists, we deliberately avoid the usual business magazine habit of industry beats. "Experts" or "pundits" don't have the answers.

Rarely do we give specific assignments. Our writers are expected, by and large, to come up with their own story ideas and then defend them to the editors. With help from researchers and statisticians they research the story, interview the chief personalities involved (including those of the competition).

Before writing it is essential that they get beyond mere descriptive material and arrive at a definite point of view on the story. Finally, the writer has to defend his point of view to one and sometimes several editors.

Coverage of business in this country is not yet up to the standards of coverage in other fields, and I think that all thoughtful business editors realize this and are trying to do something about it. This inadequacy—together with our realization that something ought to be done about it—makes journalism-in-business one of the great open-ended opportunities in writing today.

I can't think of any other part of the word business where there is so much to learn and so much to be done.

# WRITING ABOUT SCIENCE

## By Dennis Flanagan

I am supposed to comment on the word business in science and technology. First of all, let me emphasize the distinction between the two. Science is learning; technology is using. Each nourishes the other, but to blur the line between them is perilous. If a society is to survive, it must take both the long view (science) and the short (technology). As Faraday is reputed to have said when the Prime Minister looked at the induction coil and asked "What good is it?": "Someday, sir, you will be able to tax it."

The word business in science and technology has two main aspects. The first is writing by scientists and engineers. The second is writing by others about science and technology—in books, magazines, newspapers, television and radio. Both kinds of writing are in terrible shape.

When a scientist writes for other members of his discipline, he does not really write: he uses a kind of shorthand, and his specialized reader fills in the gaps. This custom is understandable, although it is sometimes a cause for mystification and even hilarity when an outsider encounters it. When a scientist writes for people outside his discipline (including scientists in other disciplines), it is quite a different matter. Often such a scientist, approaching his task with all the good will in the world, appears to be responding to motives that have little to do with whether or not he is understood. He worries: Is what I am saying properly qualified? What will Joe (his colleague) think? What will his old professor think? What will the foundation that supports his research think? Rather low on his list is: What will the reader seeking enlightenment think? One can sympathize with his predicament, but if the job of explaining to others what he does is not to fail completely, he must have considerable nerve.

Of course scientists are not really in the word business, in the sense that they are not obliged to write every day in order to get paid. I must observe, however, that if present trends continue, some day most people will be scientists and technologists. This makes it all the more compelling to consider the writer who undertakes to explain to others what scientists and technologists do.

Such writing is a pleasant occupation with an expansive future. People who are in the profession have the sensation of doing something worthwhile and of learning something, willy-nilly, as they go along. The odd part about the profession is that almost no one is going into it. Consider the fact that at *Scientific American* there are whole years when not one new or prospective college graduate walks in the door and says, "I'd like a job on the editorial staff here." Conversely, hardly a week passes that we do not receive a call from someone asking if we know a writer on science who would like to have a job, write a book, do a television script or what have you.

To be sure, when times are good it seems that there is a shortage of anyone to do any job, from housemaid to president of the company. The shortage of what are called science writers probably has to do with the fact that a writer is a general-purpose man. He is not much restricted by any specialty; the world, or at least a good piece of it, is his oyster. Accordingly it would seem somewhat difficult for a young person to decide in high school or college that he (or she) would like to make a living writing about science. Even if he knew that such an occupation existed, it would not be possible to prepare for it in the sense one prepares for a career in medicine. I am aware that there are courses of study in writing and journalism (there are even some in science writing), but no professional writer feels that such courses could in themselves have taken him very far.

After all, what is professional writing? If I may borrow a definition that the late P. W. Bridgman applied to the scientific method, it is doing your damnedest with your head. In order for a writer to do his damnedest to some effect, it is necessary for him to interest himself in everything he can, not merely attend trade school.

This is especially true of writing about science. The writing itself is just like any other writing, or should be. It is not possible for any man to master all the sciences. A writer can acquire a certain literacy in science, but beyond that he must maintain his innocence and curiosity. He can also learn some useful working principles.

Although the principles of writing are well known, it is remarkable how seldom they are mentioned. I rather suspect that most people who are aware of them are embarrassed to say anything so obvious. A few principles I like are as follows:

First, organize your piece before you write it. Then, however, do not hesitate to reorganize the organization if the actual writing exposes weaknesses in it. A colleague of mine who has taught me many things about writing once remarked to me: "A well-organized story writes itself." On the basis of experience, I can only say amen.

Second, say straight out what you mean. Don't limit yourself by some artificial scheme or try to cut some kind of fancy figure. In any case the reader will probably not know what kind of fancy figure you are trying to cut. It is sometimes said that it is a mistake to believe you can write the way you talk. I am not at all sure that is so. It certainly seems that during the past few centuries writing has evolved in the direction of sounding more and more like speech, and perhaps it should go all the way. This does not mean using casual grammar, rows of dots and incomplete sentences. It is assumed that the written word has the benefit of reflection, planning and correction.

Third, begin your piece by giving the reader a good idea of what you are going to say. This applies to any kind of prose, even when the beginning is artfully indirect, as it is in some of the most creative writing. Many intelligent people who have not done much writing make the logical assumption that the way to tell a story is to begin at A and end at Z. What this overlooks is that the reader may not wait around for Z. Every professional writer learns that he must have a strong "lead" that gives the reader a sense of what is to come, perhaps even going quickly from A to Z and then starting at a more leisurely pace all over again. Devotees of this principle are fond of an ancient anecdote about a country preacher who is asked the secret of his uncommonly effective sermons. He replies: "I tell them what I'm going to tell them, then I tell them, then I tell them what I've told them."

Fourth, suffer a little. In my own experience I have observed that many willing people underestimate the difficulty of writing well, and accordingly become discouraged and do not give the job the full measure of their ability. Even some professional writers I have known have in mind an image of some other writer, somewhere, who sits down at the typewriter with a smile on his lips and thrums away like a pianist. I am reasonably sure that such a writer does not exist. Once when Red Smith was complimented on the easy flow of his sports writing, he replied: "It all comes out in little drops of blood." Of course, some people write more easily than others, and it is possible to take the task so hard that nothing comes out at all. The crux of the matter is to approach the job with a respectful estimate of the effort it will take. This helps to eliminate a profound psychological hazard of writing.

These things hold no less for writers who write about science than for writers who write on other subjects. In fact, they may apply more forcefully to writing about science, since such writing is an effort to bridge a gap between people who do not understand one another. This is the work of those who write about science; and, as the members of our evolving society are obliged to become more specialized, who can doubt that it is a significant calling? And such writing has its own reward: the writer, if he is worth his salt, is privileged to have a ringside seat at how the whole wonderful and terrifying machine operates.

## 21

## DISTRIBUTION PROBLEMS

*By* ROBERT M. GOSHORN

The distribution of magazines to customers throughout the United States and Canada is like the distribution of any other perishable commodity, with one possible exception: with magazine subscriptions also available, many of the regular readers of a magazine are not customers of this distribution.

As a result, magazine distribution must be geared to take advantage of *impulse* as well as regular purchase. Magazines must be distributed where they will be available to prospects. They must be given exposure and displayed where they will be seen and will catch the prospect's eye. They must be promoted in a manner that creates an impulse that leads to a sale.

Magazines are sold in over 100,000 places in the United States and Canada. The term "newsstand" or "news dealer" to describe these outlets is now something of a misnomer, for today magazines are sold wherever people shop, wherever an impulse to "pick up a copy" might exist.

Distribution to these 100,000-plus outlets is accomplished through about 750 wholesalers, located in the major cities and trading areas throughout the United States and Canada. Each of these wholesalers serves anywhere from 75 dealers to a high of almost 2,000 outlets, covering areas ranging from a section of a city to the major part of several states.

The distribution begins with the establishment of the print order and the making of an allotment to each wholesaler by the publisher or national distributor, an allotment which the wholesaler in turn breaks down to allot copies to the individual dealers or outlets he serves.

Many factors are taken into consideration in the setting of the print order and in making these allotments. What has been the sales history? What is the current trend of sales? Should any seasonal adjustments be made? Are there other special considerations, such as the opening or closing of school in a college town, or the influx of tourists in resort areas during vacation periods?

Are there variations that will affect sales, such as interest in the World Series, religious holidays, local labor strikes or unusual economic conditions?

Also important is the particular issue of the particular publication. Does it contain editorial material that will have greater than average interest or appeal in a particular geographic area or among a selected group of people? Or that lends itself to special local promotion that will increase sales in a given area? Or is a "hot" item or "scoop" or timely feature expected to increase sales generally?

Normally the wholesaler will bundle together the magazines being delivered to each dealer; occasionally magazines not included in the bundle will be delivered at the same time in a "loose delivery." Depending on the nature and size of the outlet, the routeman may either just drop the bundle with the dealer, or he may take the bundle in, open it, and display the magazines on the rack for maximum sales appeal.

A primary step in good distribution is to see that the magazines are properly displayed on the racks so that individual publications can be seen and recognized, their cover lines exposed where they can be read.

This phase of distribution has become considerably more difficult during the past few years with the proliferation of magazine titles, many of them "one-shot" specialized items and comic books. The current trend is to group magazines of similar editorial content together on the rack, with many racks now marked to reserve individual sections on the rack for individual publications.

Proper display not only makes for a neater and more attractive appearance in the store, giving greater exposure and leading to greater sales, but it also makes it easier and more economical for wholesaler and dealer personnel to service the rack and keep it up-to-date.

To give additional exposure to magazines, auxiliary displays are frequently set up to take advantage of greater exposure at the checkout counter or the high traffic locations. These displays may be on additional racks set up in another section of the outlet, or may be special displays in conjunction with other merchandise in the store.

Frequently magazines (which are an above-average mark-up item for the dealer) are coupled with high-turn-over lower-margin merchandise in a display to give the dealer maximum return from a display area.

Thus, while a publication may be on sale in 100,000 outlets, it may

# MAGAZINES

have exposure in as many as 125,000 locations as additional or multiple displays are set up in supermarkets and other outlets with heavy traffic.

Studies have shown that fewer than one out of five customers in a supermarket shops at every department while he or she is in the store; the use of these auxiliary displays increases the chance of exposure for the shopper who does not visit the regular magazine department in the store, and the chance for the impulse to strike for the shopper who is "exposed" for the second or third time while in the store.

At the same time, personnel of the wholesaler, the distributor, and in many cases the publisher too, will begin promotion for that issue of the magazine to create or augment the impulse to buy. Posters are set up. Insert cards featuring special items of interest in the magazine for that display are put into the stack of magazines on display. Other special point-of-sale promotion, some received from the distributor or publisher, others locally made, is arranged.

If the issue contains features with news value, press releases are prepared for the local newspapers, radio stations, and television stations. People featured in the magazine are lined up for special appearances or interviews on radio and television programs. Arrangements are made to use open-end tapes or other promotional material supplied by the publisher.

Nor do availability and exposure end with the initial allotment. After the initial distribution of major publications, check-ups will be made during the on-sale period.

This check-up serves two purposes. Using information on previous sales trends between the on-sale date and the check-up date, it enables the distributor or publisher to estimate quite accurately what his final sale will be for that issue. At the same time, it enables the wholesaler to measure sales for individual outlets or dealers, and to make redistribution among these dealers to supply more copies where a dealer might otherwise have a sell-out and to reduce returns for those who might otherwise be over-stocked.

At the end of the on-sale period, the whole cycle starts all over again with the new current issue.

As mentioned earlier, in planning allotments, provision is made for a return allowance to insure that dealers will have copies available right up to the end of the on-sale period. These unsold copies (or "returns") are returned by the dealer to the wholesaler, who allows credit for them in the dealer's next invoice. The wholesaler in turn returns an affidavit of unsold copies (or in some cases a portion of each copy) to the distributor and is similarly given a credit in his account with the distributor.

The distribution of each issue of magazines to over 100,000 dealers is a highly complex process *aimed at giving* a perishable product with a limited sales period availability and exposure, and to create or augment the impulse to buy it. Very few people ever go out to buy a magazine or put it on the shopping list. But in the course of a year, through this distribution process, over one billion copies are sold to customers throughout the United States and Canada.

# IV
# BOOKS

22

## SUCCESS BETWEEN COVERS

*By* Joseph J. Famularo

In 1965 book sales went well over a billion dollars, an all time high. Almost twenty-nine thousand new titles were published last year. "The book business is flourishing," say Wall Streeters as book publishers merge and stock is split. But who in book publishing can define the formula for the successful book? Book publishing works strangely, but it works. Almost everyone in this field will agree: it's a wonderful world of work.

In or out of book publishing, no one questions the contribution books make to our cultural and educational advancement—our lives enriched in countless ways. Book publishing serves the public by facilitating the expression of ideas—good and bad, conventional and controversial—on subjects of every conceivable kind. It is an integral part of the free press. Book sales, which have been rising for a number of years, will continue to increase. The factors responsible for the rise in book sales in the 1950's continued to expand in the 1960's. School enrollments, representing over 50 per cent of the civilian population in the 5 to 34 age group, are responsible for a large share of the increase. Higher levels of literacy, rising personal incomes and increased leisure all provide a favorable climate for books. Export sales also should continue upward, stimulated by Government programs of the United States Information Agency and the Agency for International Development and, most importantly, increasing interest and activity on the part of U.S. publishers in foreign markets. The American Book Publishers Council has computed the percentage increases in dollar volume of sales for the period 1951-1960 as follows:

| Category of Books | Percentage Change '52-'60 |
|---|---|
| Adult trade, hardbound | plus 62.4 |
| Juvenile, $1.00 and over (retail) | plus 158.7 |
| Religious | plus 47.4 |
| Business, Science and Technology | plus 137.7 |

Book publishing is a business of great diversification, a profession, and a gamble. But it's a fascinating world; let's take a look at it.

A book publisher makes available to a general or specific public ideas in words and pictures created by an author worked over by editors, and reproduced by a printer. Broadly speaking, there are three major tasks which face a book publisher: securing and selecting manuscripts, seeing that the manuscripts are transformed into books, and promoting their ultimate use. A myriad of book subjects are published each year in the United States and it would be difficult to place each book into a distinct classification. For our purposes, the following four book "categories" should cover the majority of them.

(1) *Trade books* are those of general interest, designed for both adult and juvenile audiences, for retail bookstore sale. They include "belle lettres," novels, biographies, religious books, certain medical scientific and technical books, as well as how-to-do-it books.

(2) *Textbooks,* designed as teaching tools, are published for either basic course or supplementary and reference use in elementary and high schools, technical institutes, colleges and universities.

(3) *Reprints,* mostly paperbacks, are published for "mass market" distribution, usually at prices less than those of original publication.

(4) *Reference books* include monumental encyclopedias, handbooks, dictionaries, monographs, and abstracts published to serve specialized interests of both juvenile and adult audiences.

Book publishing is an urban industry—New York City is its mecca. I would guess that over two-thirds of the book publishing firms are in New York City and its environs. Major publishing houses, however, can also be found in Boston, Philadelphia, Chicago, and Cleveland. Although career advice might dictate "Go West, Young Man" (this may be true for the sale of books), it is usually necessary for the young man to go *East* to edit, design, manufacture, and cost-account books.

A successful publishing house, like any other successful business, must make a profit. Book publishing involves a succession of activities, each one affecting the success or failure of a given title, its profit or loss. The publisher must obtain and select a manuscript, see it through its editing phases, oversee its design and manufacture and then promote, sell, and distribute it to its intended market place.

Virtually each book must be treated as a separate product from all other books—each book requires individual attention from its editors, printers, and salesmen. The great diversity of the book business—the limitless variety of subject matter dealt with, the many different ways in which specialized markets are exploited, and the succession of activities which, added up, constitute publishing—affords a tremendous variety of jobs.

There are many, as we have said, and because of this it may be best to look at this variety of jobs according to the different functions within a publishing house.

*The general editor or sponsoring editor's* job is to obtain and select manuscripts. Many "trade" book proposals reach the editor's desk through the author's literary agent, while most textbook, scientific, or professional book projects are solicited direct by the publishers. In other cases the publisher generates his own book idea and then seeks out the proper author. In addition to evaluating manuscripts and developing with the author a book idea into manuscript form, the sponsoring editor also plays an active role in over-seeing the book's design and manufacture and collaborating in the book's overall sales plan. In large publishing firms there are several layers of general editorial responsibility which may include editor-in-chief, senior editor, associate editor, and editorial assistant. Anyone filling these jobs must have the ability to bring out the best creative talent in an author coupled with an objective eye for a manuscript's quality and marketability. A substantial financial risk is undertaken by a publishing house with each new title, and more likely than not the decision to take such a risk—"to publish or not to publish"—is made on the sponsoring editor's initial recommendation.

The *copy editor* receives the completed manuscript from the sponsoring editor and prepares it for the printer. Hours of careful copy editing are involved; typographical, grammatical, and spelling errors are corrected, confusing passages are clarified, and the manuscript is marked so that it is in literary form ready for the printer.

At the same time, the *book designer* is working with the "look" of the book-to-be from a functional and aesthetic point of view. He selects a suitable type face, designates chapter headings, page layout, and also creates the book's binding design.

For certain heavily illustrated books the *art director* combines his talents with the book designer in working on picture layout and use of other illustrations. (Compare a recently published basic biology or geography text with one published 15 years ago and see the significant changes that have occurred in book design—changes that have not only made texts far more appealing to the eye but far more readable as well.)

Today most book publishers purchase outside printing and binding services; and the *production supervisor* serves as liaison between the publisher and the printer and binders. Working with his *cost estimator*, such materials as binding cloth, paper, book jackets are ordered and all the special production problems—problems of composition, printing, engraving, etc.—are worked out.

Finally the book is born (usually several months after the manuscript has been relinquished by the author, since the editing, design, printing, and proofreading phases all take time); and then the total impact of the publisher's marketing machinery comes into play.

Promoting and selling books provides many, many jobs, such as *copywriting, promotion specialist, marketing analyst, advertising manager, school and college representative, or "traveler," bookstore salesman, and publicist.* Months before a book leaves the print shop promotional sales campaigns are planned which may include magazine and newspaper advertising, the development of selling aid for bookstore use, the preparation of direct mail advertising pieces, posters, dummy books, special interviews with columnists, radio and TV personalities and, of course, direct calls on bookstores and educators all over the country.

One of the best known jobs in the world of educational publishing is that of "the traveler." This young man, usually a college graduate, calls on educators in colleges, universities, medical schools, technical institutes, or schools at both primary and secondary levels to promote the use of his textbooks for student use. He is the chief liaison between his publisher and the academic world.

He not only "sells" books, he also keeps abreast of course trends and changes in curriculum, advising his editors of new book needs, reactions to texts currently in use, etc. He is in a good position to meet and cultivate potential authors and to scout for manuscripts developing in the field. Many college and school travelers are graduates from leading colleges and universities—and many of the leading textbook publishers develop their potential executives from this group of employees.

In trade book publishing, the sales representative calls on book stores in a given territory to discuss forthcoming titles on his publisher's "list," marketing plans, and special book promotions. He also reviews with the book store manager the store's current sales picture.

The *accounting* and *financial function* in book publishing is another natural area of career opportunity for college graduates. In effect, there is no real difference in the accounting and financial functions of book publishing than in other businesses. Most book publishers seek the business administration graduate for positions in this specialty and offer training program along management development lines.

In deciding on a career in book publishing, beware of the popular "glamour" trap. Employees of a book publisher have little chance of lunching with J. D. Salinger, John Gunther, or Truman Capote. You must remember that book publishing is a business which must be staffed not by the literati and bearded would-be authors, but by knowledgeable young men with alert, imaginative minds to work with material, men and ideas.

The ratio of professional skills required in book publishing is generally higher than that required in other businesses. If you are to work productively in book publishing you must care about books, and inevitably, therefore, about the book publisher's responsibility to society.

## THE PAPERBACK REVOLUTION

*By* WALTER B. J. MITCHELL, JR.

A paperback house today does everything that a hardcover house does, particularly on its original books. You conceive the idea, ferret out an author, edit the manuscript, revise the galleys, design the package, promote and publicize and *publish* in every sense of the word.

The differences are not in the book. To paraphrase Gertrude Stein —"A book is a book is a book." The essential difference is in the marketing techniques. Whereas trade books are distributed to 2500 outlets, 400 of which do 75 per cent of the business, paperbacks get into some 125,000 different outlets, the corner newsstand, drug stores, chain stores—you name it.

There are some 190,000 paperback titles currently in print. Sales of mass-market paperbacks have for the last several years been constant at around 300,000,000. However, if optimistic estimates come to fruition, in the educational field alone this same figure could be reached within the next three years—doubling the current market.

Mass-market publishing, as distinct from educational publishing, is the world of the best-seller, of competition for display space, and of zooming costs. The pressure of competition and readers' demand for current bestsellers is felt all around. And it has contracted the bidding for big titles to only those companies that have heavy cash backing. Five companies—Dell, Bantam, Fawcett, New American Library, and Pocket Books—now control more than 85 per cent of this "bestseller" market.

The paperback publishing business is now a "high class poker game." Publishers have been increasingly forced to bid high for titles that sometimes aren't even out in hardcover, based purely on hunches or "a feel for the book." For instance, in 1967, Dell invested two million dollars for reprinting rights to these candidates for bestsellers:

*The Games People Play*   Eric Berne
*Tai Pan*   James Clavell
*The Embezzler*   Louis Auchincloss

# BOOKS

*The Secret of Santa Vittoria*   Robert Crichton
*The Fixer*   Bernard Malamud
*Capable of Honor*   Alan Drury
*Billion Dollar Brain*   Len Deighton
*A Dandy In Aspic*   Derek Marlowe
*The Kremlin Letter*   Noel Behn
*Tinkerbelle*   Robert Manry
*Pedlock & Sons*   Stephen Longstreet
*Pleasure Of His Company*   Paul B. Fay, Jr.
*The Magus*   John Fowles

The element of risk in choosing titles for reprint, plus the challenge of "psyching" the market for the book, provide much of the fascination of paperback publication.

The largest single offer for reprints rights—a million dollars—was made by the Dell people for William Manchester's *Death of a President*. Heretofore the largest advance—which is in essence a guarantee of royalties—for fiction was $700,000 paid for *The Source*, and for nonfiction $500,000 for *In Cold Blood*. The standard royalty rate is 4 per cent of the cover price for the first 150,000 copies sold, and 6 per cent thereafter. Thus to cover a $100,000 advance, a 95¢ paperback will have to sell over a million and a half copies. The non-fiction book that so far has earned back the largest royalties is *The Rise and Fall of the Third Reich*, which recouped its advance of $400,000, plus more than $60,000 to date.

In a business where profits—and royalties—are measured in nickels and dimes, and where few books ever become million-copy sellers, advances such as these are staggering. But they reflect the fierce competition in the paperback market these days. In an industry where prestige always has meant a lot, paperback executives are desperately hunting for those few bestsellers that will draw buyers for retail book outlets to their whole line. These leading bestsellers often become loss leaders.

In a recent article in *Business Week*, Leon Shimkin, president of Pocket Books, Inc., is quoted as saying:

"There are just too many books and too many titles on the market. This gives premium value to bestsellers that can get command space—the rack position that a publisher gets in a retailer's display."

In a lead article for *The New York Times Book Review* (February 27, 1966), Pyke Johnson, Jr., editor-in-chief of Doubleday's Anchor Books and chairman of the American Book Publishers'

Council on Paperbound Publishing, told of the challenging new role of the paperback in education. Calling it the "New Eldorado," Mr. Johnson explained:

"As publishers look at the rich, new educational market, they are finding its bounty is not to be had merely for the free asking. Traditionally, it has been served by some 100 textbook publishers, of which Harcourt, Brace & World, McGraw-Hill and Ginn are typical. Their editors often spend years and millions of dollars to produce for elementary and secondary schools a "Basal text series" in such fields as literature and the social sciences. Their large forces of field representatives work constantly to obtain "adoptions" by state and city school systems.

"Virtually every one of the more than 300 firms publishing paperbacks now has its eye on some sector of the educational field. The majority, interested in the college market, have relatively little trouble reaching it.

"The elementary and secondary school market has been a more difficult nut for the publishers to crack. To comprehend the nature of this difficulty it is necessary to understand the diverse origins of the leading firms.

"Some imprints—the so-called mass-market lines like Pocket Books' Washington Square Press, Bantam, Dell, New American Library and Fawcett—began their businesses in close association with the magazine industry, relying for their distribution on the 800 or so periodical wholesalers throughout the country.

"A second group are arms of old-line trade book publishers; Doubleday's Anchor Books and Viking's Compass Books are examples of these. In general, their distribution is through the country's 5,000 or so bookstores, including college stores, which also carry hardcover books.

"A third type are the school paperback book clubs, most of them operated by Scholastic Book Services.

"The chief way a teacher may obtain a mass-market or trade paperback she wishes to use in her classroom is through a local wholesaler or bookstore."

Mr. Johnson concluded, "But throughout the country there are as yet barely a dozen places—wholesalers or jobbers—where a teacher stands a fair chance of finding adequate supplies of both mass-market and trade paperbacks."

On a subject of topical interest, paperbacks can provide rapid communication to the entire country, as was the case with Bantam's reprint of the Warren Report, which was rushed out in nearly 24 hours. A most recent case of topical publishing is *Retrial* (also Bantam), a report on the Sam Sheppard case that was on sale several days after the verdict with a final chapter discussing the new verdict.

Paperback publishing also makes it possible to reissue long out-of-print titles appealing to specialized markets such as research libraries and scholars. Because of the limited size of the market for hardcover books, the publisher may be financially unable to reissue, say, 3,000 copies of an out-of-print book, but able to break even on 50,000 paperbound copies.

In France the paperback comes first and then the hardcover. It wouldn't surprise me if this became a trend in America, too, especially for launching new novels. Initial paperback publication brings a book to its widest audience first, with the added advantage that the author doesn't have to share the advance with the hardcover house.

Book publishing as a whole, and this includes paperback publishing, differs from most industries in that a customer for any one company becomes a customer for all. We at Dell like to have as many bestselling titles in our paperback line as we can, with the full knowledge that the book buyer will be attracted to other publishers' titles as well. No matter which book is sold, publishing as a whole has gained, and what is good for any paperback publisher, in terms of sales, is good for us. The problem is to create and maintain a lively and energetic climate for reading.

To end on an optimistic note, consider the role of the paperback in tomorrow's world, as seen through the eyes of today's paperback-oriented teenagers who are better educated and more sophisticated and worldly and have created a slew of bestsellers on their own (*Catcher in the Rye, Catch-22, Lord of the Flies, Karen, The Diary of Anne Frank,* the *Tolkien* series, etc.) We will have a generation brought up on, and used to, paperbacks as well as a forthcoming generation which owns its own paperbacks from Grade One. The revolution is still in full force. The prospect of making America the best read country in the world is now a glowing reality.

24

# TEXTBOOKS AND REFERENCE WORKS

*By* E. J. McCabe, Jr.

The amount of knowledge to be communicated during the process of education increases geometrically each year.

There have been estimates that as much technical knowledge will be developed in the next 30 years as has been accumulated in the entire past history of mankind. In this country alone, we produce approximately 25,000 technical papers every week, along with 400 books and 3,500 articles.

This abundance requires basic school books to present the central core of facts, ideas and concepts of a subject, with satellite materials to cover the various aspects in depth. In addition, continual updating is required to keep the material current.

Educational publishing has been one of America's most rapid growth industries over the past 20 years. From a volume of approximately $150 million in 1950, the industry more than doubled to $350 million in 1960. By the end of 1969 the industry volume will have probably doubled again.

The discovery during World War II that many of our youth were virtually illiterate in mathematics and science inspired scholars to turn their attention to ways of improving the curriculum. The events of the late 1950's—Sputnik—hastened these efforts, and research projects were initiated in many areas of science, mathematics and the teaching of modern foreign languages.

Today curriculum studies are in progress in the social studies and English as well. The prime feature of all these studies is the emphasis on discovery of methods of learning.

Government at all levels has become more involved in education as the relationship of an educated population to the development of the economy becomes increasingly apparent. The government projects will move us toward the realization of the concept of lifelong education for all citizens.

Federal programs recently enacted by Congress provide many new opportunities for publishers—in educating pre-school children, non-literate adults, disadvantaged youths and gifted children, students

# BOOKS

in foreign countries, as well as support for research into many new approaches to subject matter.

The schools have kept pace with developments by evolving new methods of instruction and introducing new technological aids. Team teaching, nongraded classrooms, advanced placement and downward movement of subject matter have enabled the teacher to give more individual attention to students.

Programmed instruction, electronic laboratories, television, films and film-strips, records and tape recorders, slides and opaque projectors have proved to be of great value in helping students to learn by adding dimensions to the classroom experience.

Future classrooms might contain such equipment as computers and talking typewriters. Computers can provide lessons tailored to individual needs so that the student can control the speed of presentation in accordance with his own progress. What is essential for all of the new types of methodology and technology is the "software" to utilize its full potential.

And here is where the educational publisher is the key. Already, they are producing materials to complement the innovative practices in the schools. The ethnic and racial diversity and the contributions of minority groups to the development of the American nation are receiving more coverage.

More books are being produced for use in adult basic education. These books are geared for low skill achievement but are high in adult interest motivation. The teaching of English as a second language is recognized by publishers as a separate discipline, and materials are being developed for this subject. The new federal programs have inspired new materials, and the curriculum study groups have required them.

There are multi-level texts to compensate for individual differences. A history textbook is produced in four individual volumes for easier student use. A weekly supplement accompanies an economics text in order to keep data current. Systems of instruction are increasingly becoming part of the publishers catalog. Such additional aids as filmstrips, motion pictures, tapes and discs are offered with the textbook. Science kits accompany textbooks in an elementary science series.

Paperbound books are of increasing importance as supplementary aids and as central instructional tools. One important advantage is their ability to make current knowledge and thinking and current art forms available to children and youth immediately.

The educational publisher is an essential ingredient in the development of the appropriate instructional needs of today. The experience he has acquired in producing a book that children can understand and from which a teacher can instruct is vital.

The publisher most often secures the author, or team of authors, to write the manuscript. He provides an editor, either from his staff or an outside consultant, with the knowledge of the subject matter and the grade level it is designed for. He provides the staff members who research the curriculum requirements of the schools and determine what type of book the schools will want.

When the book presents a new approach to the subject matter, such as the "new mathematics," the publisher will often organize seminars and workshops for the teachers to explain its use, and the various classroom applications.

In order to perform its function properly, the educational publishers require the leadership and talent of highly skilled, trained professionals. Jobs in educational publishing divide into several categories.

First, there is the product creation and development category where educational products are planned, written, edited, tested and printed or otherwise manufactured. Whereas the need for writers and editors is obvious, many educational publishers now employ psychologists to supervise testing and quality control programs, as well as personnel trained in business administration with specialities in manufacturing and procurement.

Another major category is product distribution. This includes sales and sales management, advertising and promotion as well as the product logistics—the warehousing, inventory control and shipping of the materials. In the United States the educational establishment is not centralized, and 30,000 independent districts operate schools.

A major responsibility of the educational publisher is to communicate with these many units to explain the products and product characteristics which will enable the school or school system to perform its mission. Doing this properly not only requires the usual skills of sales and sales management and advertising and promotion, but also requires a level of professionalism—since communication is primarily with a professionalized audience.

In educational publishing it is extremely rare today for a publisher to "accept" an unsolicited manuscript and publish it. Much more planning is required to determine the role the product is to fill in the schools, the characteristics necessary to fulfill that role properly and the best methods of obtaining those characteristics in the products.

In general, this requires highly professionalized, knowledgeable planning personnel within the educational publishing company. But many outside consultants and members of the educational profession are also utilized. Very often the planning must take place years before the introduction of the products, and the educational publisher must analyze not only the existing curriculum, but the trends, in order to be sure that by the time the work is published, it is not out of date.

An interesting example of the magnitude of this problem took place in our own company when seven years ago we decided to publish a new elementary school encyclopedia, *The New Book of Knowledge*.

The first step was, of course, to analyze the current and emerging curriculum patterns of the elementary schools to determine exactly what characteristics a modern elementary school encyclopedia should have.

However, a compilation of a 20-volume encyclopedia containing over six million words, 85,000 index entries, and 22,000 illustrations, with articles written by over 1,200 contributors, is a prodigious task, and if done properly, takes time.

The curriculum analysis and editorial policies for the new encyclopedia which were carried on and created in 1959 had to anticipate the educational curricula requirements for the elementary school of 1966, because it was not until October of that year that the first volumes of the new encyclopedia went into schools.

In absolute numbers, the size of the educational establishment is tremendous. The total number of students in public and private schools and colleges during the 1965-66 school year is 54.5 million. One Congressional witness recently stated: "The American economy was built around the railroads in the last half of the nineteenth century, around the automobile in the first two-thirds of this century, and it will be built around education in the balance of this century." Education now takes 6.7 per cent of the gross national product. The educational budget is expected to rise to about $48.8 billion for 1969-70.

Educational publishing is aware of its responsibilities and opportunities to work with the new trends in education and provide whatever tools are required in the classroom to give each student the most meaningful and comprehensive education.

25

## SCHOLARLY PUBLISHING

### By Chester Kerr

Strung across the United States, and into Canada and Mexico, lie some 70 university publishing enterprises—scholarly book publishers attached to all kinds of universities, large and small, state and private. Today they occupy a significant place in the American book publishing scene, as well as in the apparatus of research and higher education. In a word, they are the vehicles of American scholarship, bearing its results to academic and general readers throughout the world.

The original models for these enterprises were established, of course, at Oxford and Cambridge several hundred years ago. American counterparts first made their appearance in the 19th century, at Cornell, Johns Hopkins, Columbia, and Chicago, when the German concept of graduate work first took hold. In the early 1900's, university publishing was taken up at the state universities, notably California and Michigan, and at leading private institutions across the land—Stanford, Princeton, Yale, Harvard.

In the 1920's Oklahoma, North Carolina, Wisconsin, Minnesota, Illinois, Washington all spawned presses. The rush was on and in the two decades after World War II, as higher education exploded in the land, the number quickly doubled. No major institution of learning in the United States has failed to add to its body of scholars and its library the third ingredient: a publishing arm.

So it is that today one out of every twelve new books published in the U.S. each year bears a university press imprint; more notably, one out of every seven books currently in print bears a university label. Their sales dollar volume has multiplied five times in less than twenty years. Their managements and staffs have evolved from local amateur beginnings into highly qualified professional publishing teams The librarian or the faculty member who helped launch the press has returned to his job; the director of a press today is more likely than not to have come from trade or textbook publishing, although the field is now beginning to attract college graduates in increasing numbers.

A university press is like any other book publishing house in its departmental organization. There is an editorial department charged with seeking manuscripts, with judging submissions, and with "editing" accepted manuscripts. "Editing" may mean the technical job of copy-editing, that is, making certain that punctuation and capitalization and the use of proper names are correct and consistent and that footnotes are accurate—or it may mean the more creative task of assisting the author to condense or otherwise improve his style and the organization of his material.

Scholarly writers are like all writers: they often need help. A capable editor may often be instrumental in converting a poor or an ordinary manuscript into a first-class one that will bear its message farther and wider. To do so, he must know something of the subject in hand. He must know how to organize material and to write. He must, above all, have that essential ingredient: sympathy. Or call it compatability. It's what it takes to sit down alongside an author, himself an expert and maybe edgy, yet needing help, and in hours or days guide him to better construction and expression. It is a noble yet often thankless task—like teaching or obstetrics.

Editors in university presses often possess higher degrees—M.A.'s or even doctorates. The two youngest editors at the Yale University Press are fresh from the Yale Graduate School, having decided, after all, in favor of publishing instead of teaching or scholarship. An advanced degree is not absolutely necessary, but it helps. It gains respect from an author and if often leads to successful specialization: Yale divides its editorial responsibilities into the areas of humanities, arts, social sciences, and physical sciences, for example.

When a manuscript is ready for the printer, the typographer and the manufacturing department take over. The design of books requires special training in the graphic arts. At the Yale Press, the four designers are all graduates of either the Yale Art School or the Rhode Island School of Design. Production personnel are also specialists, although here they may learn on the job. A taste for the problems of composition, printing and binding is desirable, if not actual plant experience.

With the finished book in hand comes the problem of distribution. Next after editorial work, the popular entry point into university press publishing is through sales and promotion. Scholarly publishers do not do as much direct selling these days as they one did when they first copied commercial book sales techniques.

Calling on Brentano's or a Doubleday bookstore with a satchel full of samples from the forthcoming seasonal list is a practice still employed by trade houses, but in recent years university presses have more closely identified the outlets for their wares and so concentrate their efforts on college stores, libraries, and scholars themselves, often through direct mail. It is more important for a university press sales representative to visit Ann Arbor than Detroit—and the University of Chicago Bookstore is likely to sell more of his output than any other Chicago bookstore. But he isn't on the road for an extended time and his office work is far more valuable.

The promotion of a book includes the preparation of advertising, publicity, catalogs, direct mail pieces, and all the other wrinkles used to insure that a book reaches its market. In the case of most university press books, this means a very special market—requiring rifle aim, not the broad shotgun effort needed with a novel or a book about John F. Kennedy. Searching out the audience for *The Sharing of Power In a Psychiatric Hospital* or *Church and State In French Colonial Louisiana* or *Something of Great Constancy, a study of Midsummer Night's Dream*, requires a particular skill and no experience with pushing John Hersey's new novel or William Shirer's book on the Nazis. The skill includes a familiarity with academic journals, with identifiable library interests, with categorical mailing lists. It also requires the ability to convey the contents of a volume of limited appeal succinctly and accurately to the few who will "must have it" or may possibly want it. The language of the university world is more useful in such a task than any picked up at Foote, Cone, and Belding.

Business-minded? Computer-conscious? Keen on administration? This end of book publishing is growing in complexity and attraction and suits anyone who finds life in a small business appealing, as opposed to a corporation or a mass-media outfit or a government agency. The records must be kept, the business end of the act of publication must proceed effectively. This is to say that books must be warehoused and shipped, invoices must be sent, bills rendered, cash received, collections made, and the whole shebang accounted for. Used to be that the parent institution's business office took care of these things. Now most university presses handle their own transactions and keep their own records—and so need competence of this kind from young men to whom that kind of occupation holds satisfactions.

The greatest satisfaction accorded to anyone employed at a university press is, by common agreement among most of the inhabitants of this branch of book publishing, the attraction of a university community. Cambridge, Mass., or Berkeley, California, (despite Governor Reagan) or Austin, Texas, or Urbana, Illinois, have assets which for many outweigh the attractions (not to mention the air pollution) of Boston, San Francisco, Dallas, or Chicago—and besides those environments, nice to visit, are all near at hand. These assets include the obvious benefits of any cultural center—lectures, concerts, exhibitions, theatre—plus exposure to the intellectual and social fement in which any lively campus is knee-deep these days. The outcries on civil rights and Vietnam heard across our land have been heavily college-oriented, and so they should be. And when it comes to hanging an effigy, there's often the governor when one tires of the president.

But most of all, the American university today contains, at all levels, people—people worth talking to, making friends with, living among. The opportunity to join such a community of people has never been greater than today for any young graduate who wants to enter book publishing and who is willing to leave New York City to others. The field is growing, even to the point of boom; the pay and the benefits are also on the increase. And there's lots of room at the top.

## 26

## PUBLISHING FOR CHILDREN

### By SETH AGNEW

Historically, children's book publishing is new. The first children's book department in publishing houses came into being in the early 1920's. The first children's rooms in libraries were started at about the same time.

Not 50 years later, U.S. book publishing and U.S. libraries are world-renowned for the quantity and quality of their offerings for children. Although some of the children's books published in this country are imports from abroad or translations of books already published there, including a substantial larding of English books, our own writers and illustrators have developed an expertise in the field that is generally acknowledged. Our system of children's libraries is unparalleled in any other country, and has now expanded to include not only public libraries but also school libraries and classroom collections.

There are two main streams of children's publishing in the U.S. One is mass-market, with low-priced books distributed through toy stores, variety stores, and high-volume merchandising outlets. For the most part, the books distributed in the mass-market are multicolored as to illustration, big in page size, glossy in appearance, although series books, such as *Nancy Drew* and *The Hardy Boys*, also have their major sale in the mass-market.

The other kind of juvenile publishing is the so-called "trade" publisher. These books are higher-priced; their packaging is less elaborate. They sell in bookstores and in well-developed book sections of department stores. Trade children's books, too, form a large part of the collections of libraries and classrooms.

Much of the sale of trade children's books is from the backlist—books published in years gone by, sometimes as much as half a century ago. According to some estimates, while the sale of adult books is about 40 percent to 50 percent new publications, in children's books the backlist sales may run as high as 85 percent. In partial explanation of this phenomenon, one has only to consider that the adult reader remains adult for years and is more interested in finding something newly published. Every year, on the other hand, a new class of children "find" Pooh, and Mary Poppins, and the Hobbit.

It is in school libraries and classrooms that the most recent growth in the children's book business has been found. Modern pedagogical theory holds that, in addition to the textbook at the core of the curriculum, an integral part of the course is supplementary reading of the very kind of trade juveniles that children's book editors have been publishing for years.

The Federal Elementary and Secondary Education Act of 1966, making millions of dollars available to states to pass along to their school systems for the development of their curriculums, their facilities, and their libraries, was only the climax of legislative action on all levels—community, state, and federal—which has provided the funds to build up public libraries and school collections.

It seems safe to say that about 80 to 85 percent of all juvenile sales end up with institutional customers. This compares with a probable 60 to 65 percent of adult hardbound books absorbed by the institutional market.

While backlist is an important part of the sales picture, in order to get books for the backlist children's book publishers must make a strong effort each year to find the kind of new books to publish that have the potential to become backlist.

Today's children's books are mostly aimed at readers up to 12 or 14 years old. There was once a strong market for teenage romances and adventure stories, but this is now dwindling, partly because teenagers are more sophisticated, partly because the level of reading ability has gone up.

Nowadays, between the ages of 11 and 14, most children graduate from books written specifically for children to the kinds of books which libraries sometimes classify as "young adult": books by Agatha Christie or Allistair MacLean, and other books not usually thought of as children's books.

A substantial part of the publishing program of the trade publisher is in picture-books for the pre-schooler and for kindergarten through the third grade.

For older children there are books with more text to read. From 8 to 12 years of age the child rapidly develops his reading facility and learns to read books of increasing complexity. This is a time when children are likely to read omniverously, which is pleasant for the publisher; perhaps a little harder is the fact that at the same time the child is developing critical faculties and is demanding better and better books.

The most common fault with much of the writing that is submitted to children's book publishers is an apparent assumption on the part of many adults that children are somehow dim-witted, not to say gullible. Take a simple narrative, so the theory seems to go, add an improving moral, gloss the whole thing over with a veneer of doggerel, and the result will be a children's book. One often wonders what recollections of their own childhoods the holders of this theory must have.

Nor is there any reason to assume that children will not respond to good artwork and good illustrations. Perhaps they will respond better to such imaginative work as that of Maurice Sendak, say, or Evaline Ness, than to brightly colored, animated-cartoon art.

The first requirement of children's book publishers and editors, then, is a clear look at children, perhaps an honest appraisal of their own childhood, of children they may meet around them. *High Wind In Jamaica* is perhaps a truer view of children than *The Bobbsey Twins*.

Children may not be able to read as fast as adults, may not have as large a vocabulary, may not have as wide a range of background information, but they are often quite intelligent and will resent being written down to and patronized just as much at the age of 8 as they will at the age of 20.

Since so much of the market for children's books is institutional, publishers and editors need to be familiar with the needs of schools and libraries, with the latest developments in education. They need to have at least an aquaintance with the normal curriculum, so that those books which may have supplementary use are right in format and style for the age and grade of the potential reader.

American history, for example, is usually taught in fifth grade, again in eighth grade, and once again in eleventh grade. A biography of Abraham Lincoln might be of interest at any one of these levels, but it would be different in appearance, in editorial tone, in kind and amount of illustration at each of these levels.

Sales promotion and advertising of children's books differs somewhat from adult books because, again, the market is so largely schools and libraries. In point of fact, the children's book publisher hardly ever comes into direct contact with the child who is the ultimate consumer, for in both retail sales and the institutional market the initial purchase is made by adults. Grandparents, aunts and uncles, visiting friends of the family are thought to be the major purchasers of juveniles in bookstores; librarians, of course, supervise the purchase of children's books for their market.

They have developed complicated and efficient systems for evaluation of books for purchase. Proper presentation of sample books to the evaluating groups and reviewing bodies is essential to the sale of children's books in their market. And proper advertising in the media which will reach the librarian and teacher is also important.

Traditionally children's book editors and managers of children's book departments have been, like teachers and librarians, women. The picture is changing, however. As the children's book field becomes larger and more complex, as the need for competent administrators, for imaginative editors and art directors increases, it becomes increasingly necessary to hire good people, whether men or women, to fill the job openings.

In publishing, in the last five years, the number of men in promotion, in administration, and in editing has increased noticeably. The trend seems not likely to reverse itself.

## 27

## THE BUSINESS SIDE

*By* Alfred C. Edwards

To Henry Holt, who founded Holt, Rinehart and Winston back in 1866, when he was only 25, monetary considerations were not the first concern. When pressed to discuss finances by his bookkeeper, he replied, "We are in business to sell books, not to keep them." In later years he was also fond of quoting his author, Robert Frost on "The Hardships of Accounting."

*Never ask of money spent*
*Where the spender thinks it went.*
*Nobody was ever meant*
*To remember or invent*
*What he did with every cent.*

Although the publishing of books is still not solely a "business" in the usual sense of the word, the publisher who does not know, respect and follow closely the rules of economics and finance would today have a very short-lived and unhappy career.

Publishing's success now requires that the same firm have within it those with a keen sense of future trends and tastes—men who can spot a work of art in literary form and convert the material into an appropriate format for its special market: men who must satisfy the exacting standards set for those who would manage a modern growth company.

Today those highly competitive publishing growth stocks on the New York Stock Exchange represent companies staffed at the top with anything but dreamy literary types. These companies are now quite complex and are more than likely managed by a balanced team of professional specialists who are constantly aware that for best results their vocation and avocation had better be one.

They may still share the stimulation of association with highly creative artists, but they must also have a realistic sense of the very necessary balance between art and profit. The accountant's skills must be always present, but not too openly intrusive.

When I joined Holt 21 years ago, after years as a banker, the company's total sales amounted to slightly less than $2 million. Today that figure is $70 million—an example of the rapid growth in book publishing. I started as business manager and treasurer, but very shortly became executive vice president in charge of operations.

At that time there were no formal procedures, manuals or controls for the running of the business. I had formerly been accustomd to a very precise business experience, but it was several years before I could apply these methods at Holt to my satisfaction.

At that time there were not many well-run companies in the book publishing business on which to draw for practical experience. Many of the companies were still family-owned or controlled and were run by the whim of the owner or two or three non-business type men, whose preoccupation had been wholly with the editorial or sales aspects of the companies' operations. Many of them were actually anti-business in their attitude.

Even today with more sophisticated management, there are still large areas within the book publishing industry where an inflexible posture could defeat the very purposes of the close association with creative writers.

For instance, a publisher may come to expect the publication of a very important book at a particular time. But the author may not finish the book for a year a year or two later than his original contract terms required. Then too, the work he produces may be much longer or shorter, much better or much worse for sales, than the publisher had hoped for. Thus we may never be able to budget each season's sales down to the last book and the last sales dollar.

However, the large multi-departmental publisher of today spreads his risk over 150 to 1,000 new publications each year. His editors and literary scouts, working one to five years ahead of publication, keep a steady flow of manuscripts available for the future. Each year's publications are then worked into a forecast jointly prepared by editors, sales managers and budget director. Standard costs are applied to each project when the manuscript first comes into the house. As it is edited, designed and made ready for the press, its variable dimensions are interpreted into cost factors. A retail price is set and the promotion and sales departure does its best to spread its distribution widely.

In the field of fiction and non-fiction an estimate of sales is often difficult to prepare. No one can be exactly sure of how the public will react to an author's work.

It is often said that publishing a book of this type is like opening a show on Broadway. This form of publication, known as trade books, while perhaps the most demanding artistically, is also the most risky and usually least rewarding in profits.

The development of large-scale teaching-material firms, commonly called textbook publishers, provides the schools and colleges with specific materials for study. This type of publishing involves the use of considerably more capital investment, a great deal more time in which to develop the product, sell it and collect the proceeds, than is the case with the so-called trade book publisher.

Because of this very large investment and the long waiting period for an adequate return, which sometimes extends to five years, very few text publishers have started in this country in the past 30 years. In fact, the trend in recent time has been to fewer but larger companies of this type.

This lack of new firms starting in business places somewhat of a premium on the more successful existing textbook companies when large organizations wish to enter the educational publishing field through the merger route. The trend toward mergers in this industry has continued over the past fifteen years and more recently, some large text publishers have been acquired by IBM, Xerox, General Electric, RCA, Ratheon and other large electronically-oriented companies.

During the past twenty years there has been a tremendous cultural and educational upheaval in our country and in many other places throughout the world.

All this activity has made for the considerable boom in book publishing which seems to be continuing unabated. In fact, the pace has been accelerated in the last few years by the availability, in our country, of federally-sponsored programs for the purchase of many materials for schools and colleges, from pre-kindergarten to adult education courses.

This growth phenomenon has attracted a great many men from varying professions who, prior to 20 years ago, were not sought out to staff publishing firms. We now have approximately one-third of the personnel of the larger firms taken up with various service aspects of the business. In this category of jobs are those of running the whole financial aspects of the company, its inventory control, its production, its art design of books and products, its warehousing, transportation of books and many other specialty positions.

In addition, about another third of the force is made up of those who work on editorial programs and another third in the selling and marketing aspects of the company's products. Because of the interesting work in which personnel becomes involved in many of the positions, publishers have been blessed with being able to secure high-type, dedicated and unusually well qualified applicants.

The investment market has also singled out the textbook industry as an unusually well qualified one to resist the cyclical effect of economic swings in general business conditions. Education and self-improvement go on in good times and bad.

In recent years most of the larger companies have developed rapidly growing international departments which export books and other learning materials to foreign countries. English as a second language has taken over in almost every country in the world. This, together with the demand for much more sophisticated teaching products, makes many nations turn to the United States for their books and supplies.

The larger companies have set up agencies or branches in foreign countries and have sales representatives who cover most civilized nations. The future opportunities for sustained expansion are very good in the case of the larger firms engaged in export.

The size of the total industry in the United States is somewhat in excess of the $2 billion figure. The diversity of cultural products and their uses is multiplying and this sales figure is estimated to more than double in the next ten years. With such growth it will be seen that growth opportunities for employees and stockholders far exceed those in most industries.

Were he alive today, I am sure Henry Holt would find much to criticize in terms of the emphasis on modern business management practices, but he would also recognize the need to plan for even further changes in the future.

## 28

## CHALLENGES AND OPPORTUNITNES

### By F. L. RODGERS

John Diebold, the prophet of automation, is said to have in his office a Charles Addams cartoon showing two caterpillars watching a butterfly fluttering in the distance; a flight so exciting that it prompts one caterpillar to remark to the other, "You'll never get me in one of those things."

This unsettling commentary gives one pause, especially when charged with the responsibility of advising prospective college graduates why they should go into and what they can expect from book publishing—a business so dynamic and volatile that few in it are intrepid enough to make any categorical statements about its future.

Certainly book publishing today offers unique career opportunities for a variety of reasons. First, it is the industry at this point in time that is truly all things to all men. With decades of rich traditions that no one really would like to or ever will entirely forget, its thinking has suddenly become as space-age oriented as the science fiction novels it brought to public attention. Pronouncements that the book is doomed as an effective media proliferate while, to point out the obvious, these statements are published and receive their widespread dissemination in book form.

The breadth of the publishing industry today stretches the imagination. John Galbraith places bookmakers in the category with service stations and laundries, as far as their stage of organizational development is concerned; yet an old-line publishing house sells for $250,000,000 to a major corporation. Admittedly, there are publishers whose development has not markedly progressed since the twenties, and $250,000,000 sales are rare. But these extremes serve to set the outer boundaries between which the rest of book companies will fall.

These companies include the publicly held corporation successfully competing for its share of the investor's dollar on Wall Street, and the small independent publisher who frequently has an impact on the publishing scene—and for that matter on the American scene—far out of proportion to its size. Lastly, there are medium-size family firms who, due to the recent expansion of the book market, are quickly changing their method of operating and outlook: by going public or, at minimum, becoming extremely sophisticated in their business approach.

Recognizing that many new problems are a result of pressures developing from technological and educational dynamics, publishers are becoming keenly aware that they must have intelligent, highly trained personnel who are willing to continue self-education and training. Thus salaries are becoming competitive where they were once clearly substandard. Company-supported formal education is becoming more common, too, and advancement is more closely matched to performance and training than at any time in the past.

Publishing opportunities fall into four broad categories: editorial, marketing, which includes promotion, sales and advertising; production; and business, which includes finance, administration and manufacturing.

*Editorial.* The editorial department selects manuscripts to be published and puts them into publishable form. This involves reading and making decisions about manuscripts; author contact; copy editing, which can range from simply marking the manuscript for the printer to making editorial suggestions; a great deal of coordination with other departments. In very small houses an editor and his secretary/assistant may do all these jobs; in large firms they are of course divided among many people. In either case, the job of the editorial secretary provides a good vantage point for learning the mechanics of the business while acquiring skills and experience. The secretary will handle an editor's reports and correspondence and perform other specifically secretarial duties; often she also reads manuscripts, reads proof, performs other editorial tasks which teach her a great deal.

Another good starting job is that of editorial assistant, which entails the evaluation of manuscripts and the handling of copy as it advances through the production stages. These jobs are available largely to those with a good background in English.

Prospective editorial candidates will sometimes be told that they should get some practical commercial experience such as working in a bookstore to balance their academic training. It's not bad advice, and something that I recommend to anyone who has trouble getting placed.

*Marketing.* The marketing function includes promoting, municizing, advertising and selling the company's books. This requires presenting the books to customers—retail bookstores, jobbers, and institutional representatives in high schools, colleges and public libraries; writing copy for advertisements and publicity releases; liaison with other media such as television, magazines, newspapers; and lastly the rapidly developing field of data processing as it relates to marketing.

Naturally there are more openings as sales trainee than any other. Because of the broad experience this offers it may lead to other areas of publishing—the best example being the frequent progression of salesman to editor in the college text field. For those interested in travel the attractiveness of the sales job should be apparent.

*Publicity.* With regard to publicity and promotion jobs, I would strongly advise those highly motivated to get into this field to accept any reasonable openings they can find. Advancement is often rapid, there is a tendency to make organizational changes to meet the talents of particular employees, and the long-term prospects in an exciting field are excellent.

Again, a secretarial position offers a wonderful chance to gain experience with promise of being promoted into new areas.

*Business.* Jobs available in the business department range from finance and accounting to personnel administration and office management. Business degrees or some training in business subjects is essential for financial and accounting jobs, and the publishing field offers a rare opportunity to those having this training. Long neglected by publishers, financial analysis and modern scientific management techniques are now recognized to be the invaluable tools they have been for much of American industry, making this an ideal time to begin a career.

Personnel administration and office management are at a similar stage of development. A special major or degree is not necessary, and these jobs offer an opportunity to get into an interesting field that is itself starting to mature.

*Production.* The production function includes everything from inventory control to art work. Those artistically inclined will find a highly challenging career in book design, for which some formal training in graphics is required. Book production personnel have one of the most challenging jobs in the business, serving as intermediaries between the editor and manufacturer (publishers usually contract the actual composition, printing and binding to companies who operate exclusively in this field). Frequently companies will assist a trainee in getting some formal training while beginning in this area.

There is one development worthy of mention. In the past many people have been reluctant to go into jobs in this category, fearing overspecialization. While this may have been true at one time, it no longer applies. The computer, more than anything else, through its development of information systems, has made the relationship between all departments—for example, between production and finance —so close that it is unlikely that an employee in one department could properly administer his job without considerable knowledge of the others. The trend is unmistakable, and most apparent in the case of jobs in the business department.

Not unlike the periods when railroads and automobiles dominated the business and social scene, the knowledge industry is at the dawn of a role in American life that will exceed in total effect anything that has come before it. Being part of a development such as this is both exciting and extraordinarily rewarding.

29

## IMPLEMENTING IDEAS

### By WALTER A. STALTER

One of the most pressing requirements that has resulted from the "science explosion" of the last 25 years is the requirement for effective communication between the scientist (or engineer) and his fellow workers and, perhaps more frequently, between the scientist and his using public.

Furthermore, many billions of dollars are being spent every year on scientific research; obviously, the results of this effort must be known.

It is in this potential 20th century version of Babel that the technical writer must toil.

Essentially, the technical writer is responsible for documenting the progress and results of scientific/technical (the scientist and engineer unsmilingly insist on the distinction) research and development. This documentation can take many forms. It includes proposals, reports, manuals, design and test specifications and procedures, brochures and other sales literature, motion pictures, and visual aid presentations.

Let us look at a hypothetical, but typical, *proposal preparation activity* and concentrate on the role of a technical writer in this activity, which, I might add, many writers feel is certainly the most interesting and the most challenging of all types of technical publications efforts.

Before any scientific group can begin its research, it must have adequate funding. Often the source of funds is the Government. Assume that the Government has recognized the need for a specific piece of equipment—for example, a satellite-borne camera system capable of supplying high resolution photographs of the surface of the moon.

The Government will then request that a number of companies submit proposals for this equipment, and they will supply each company with a detailed list of the specific requirements for the equipment involved. These specifications will generally delineate not only technical, but financial and management requirements as well.

As soon as we receive the request for a proposal, we will form a proposal team consisting of individuals with all the skills required to respond intelligently to the specifications that the Government has given to us. A key member of this proposal team is the technical writer.

The proposal is essentially an argument for our performing this particular task for the Government. We contend that we thoroughly understand the problems involved and are best equipped to solve them—and this proposal proves it. Thus, the writer's first task will be to assist the proposal team manager in forming an outline for our argument that assures that each area of interest (as specified by the Government in their request for the proposal) is covered adequately and, most important, presents the most logical order or argument. Once the outline is complete, the technical writer must prepare a proposal schedule.

It is inevitable in a situation where the Government has specified a proposal submittal date, that the schedule will be as "tight" as humanly possible—sometimes "tighter."

The writer, then, must see that the schedule allows the proposal team as much time as possible to "engineer" the problem, while still leaving sufficient time for publications to produce a high quality book. Obviously the proposal writer must be thoroughly familiar with all phases of the publications process.

After the proposal outline and schedule have been completed, the actual writing can begin.

In a relatively complex system such as a satellite-borne high-resolution camera, there will be many major areas of technical interest—mechanical devices, electrical control systems, the optical system itself, structural and thermal considerations, test and alignment equipment, and, in each case, the analysis to support these tasks. In addition, cost data and program planning for each phase of the proposed program must be provided.

Assignments will go out to a number of key people, each of whom will in turn be supported by other personnel, to generate the proposal material in the specific area of interest.

With the writing of the proposal underway, a whole new set of problems arises for the technical writer.

In any intelligent proposal effort, there will be considerable coordination between all of the key people responsible for specific major areas of interest; an overall design approach will be agreed upon as soon as possible, and each of the members of the proposal team will work with the rest of the team to insure consistency of the design approach.

Yet, even with reasonably effective communications within the proposal team, inconsistencies will arise. I personally know of a case where the group designing a specific piece of equipment was not "tuned in" with the people designing the test facility for the same equipment. The result—they could not get the equipment into the test facility; the doors were too small.

The problem is, I think, further compromised by the extreme complexity and sophistication of modern day equipment (a multitude of specialists in a wide variety of skills is required to propose a single piece of equipment) and the somewhat unfortunate, albeit necessary, tendency towards specialization in the education of scientists and engineers (an increasingly common response to technical inquiries today is "you'd better ask so and so; that's his field—not mine"). Inevitably, then, each area of the proposal will be written almost as though it were an entity in itself.

The technical writer will be one of the few people who will read the complete proposal, chapter for chapter, word for word, and so he must be alert to mutually contradictory solutions to the same problem. Certainly, the writer cannot be expected to solve problems of technical conflict, but he must assist the proposal manager in locating them as soon as possible to avoid wasting valuable hours of engineering effort.

In reviewing the proposal, the writer must also assure that there is what might be called "technical balance." If a particular system is optically very sophisticated, but comparatively straightforward electrically, then the optical system should probably be covered in considerably more detail than the electrical system. There should be a similar balance throughout the entire proposal.

The first steps completed, the technical writer must now undertake the considerable task of copy rewrite. It is an unfortunate fact that a vast number of engineers are notoriously bad writers; indeed, many of them will freely admit (almost boast) that they always have trouble "putting their ideas into words."

The writer must "translate" the proposal into clear, concise, effective English. Nobody can evaluate a proposed solution to a particular problem if they cannot determine what that solution is.

Rewriting will likely be the most time-consuming of all the technical writer's tasks. The rewriting requires that the technical writer maintain close communications with the responsible engineers to insure that he does not vitiate what he hopes to improve.

An effective proposal is not simply a bound collection of a number of inputs from various individuals; rather, it must be a unified, consistent, logical presentation of an argument. Ideally, the proposal should be the articulate voice of a single entity—the bidding company. Only effective rewriting can achieve this effect.

A good proposal will be a balanced blend of text and graphics. Thus, in addition to the schedule, outline, and writing problems with which the technical writer must contend, he will be expected to advise the proposal team on the most effective form of graphics to include in the book. The writer, then, must be thoroughly familiar with the capabilities of the publications department's technical illustrators, industrial designers, and photographers.

Finally, all the draft material—text, engineering sketches, finished drawings from the drafting boards, graphs, tabular material and photographs—will be brought together and, hopefully, approved by the proposal manager and the company management. The writer will now release this informal but complete package to the editing section for a thorough review.

The writer will work closely with the editing section, which controls and coordinates copy preparation. The editors will make a final check for technical content, format, grammar, spelling, and—where applicable, conformance to specifications. Work will be distributed from this section to typing, proofing, technical illustrating and photography. When this work is returned to the editors, they will assemble and deliver a complete package to the book layout section, where all the pieces are put together. Next, it is back to the editing sections and the proposal manager and technical writer for final checks, then to printing, and finally to the customer.

The extent of the writer's involvement in the preparation of any technical document, such as the proposal I have just described, is a variable depending on many factors—time, the writer's experience, the nature of the company's work.

The most basic factor in determining the extent of the writer's involvement in the preparation of technical documents is the educational background of the writer himself. There is little point here debating whether the best technical writer is the scientist who learns to write or the trained writer who learns science. The answer to this question cannot be a generalization; rather, the answer lies with the individual himself—whether he be a physics major or an English major.

A better approach would be for me to describe the many and varied skills and talents that we expect to find in the technical writer. First and foremost, he must obviously be a "good writer," a skill achieved only through years of study of great writers, an awareness and appreciation of their techniques, and the constant practice of the art of writing itself. In addition, the writer must be sufficiently competent technically to deal intelligently with scientists and engineers.

The writer must have sufficient grasp of the basics to be able to talk with these people (much as a reporter during an interview), learn from them exactly what it is they are trying to accomplish, and to then put these ideas effectively into words and graphics. At the same time, the writer must be conversant with all the skills that will go together to produce the end product—a book.

It is axiomatic that, while the technical writer is expected to be pretty well versed in all areas of technology, the engineer on the other hand, is blissfully unaware of publications techniques. Thus, the writer will be expected to work with structural engineers, for example, to determine how best to present a view of the equipment he is proposing.

As you can see, the writer, bridging the gap between scientist and artist, is indeed a man for all occasions.

He is in the happy position of being able to learn from both the scientist and the artist. The writer can, according to his own talents, interests, and initiative, direct his career in many directions. Through continued communication with scientific personnel and self-education (either formal or informal), the writer can certainly become more technically proficient; many technical manual writers exhibit this desire to further their technical knowledge.

Other writers might perhaps choose to concentrate on fiscal aspects of publications, and thus will work primarily in budgeting and scheduling large documentation efforts (the documentation budgets for large programs can involve as much as a million dollars). Certainly, the wide range of skills in any publications department presents a real challenge to the interested writer.

Perhaps I have made the technical writer appear more of a "superman" than he actually is; but I certainly believe that anyone who has the combination of the skills and the talents I have described is indeed unique.

The good technical writer is a rare commodity, much in demand, and the rewards are correspondingly high. It is a comparatively young profession, and if you have the talents, the opportunities for advancement are virtually unlimited—it's up to you.

# V
# LIBRARIES

30

## PROVIDING INFORMATION

### By Donald H. Hunt

Today's library, a dynamic institution, is the vital core of the information and communications overload. Without the library there could be no expansion of educational or scientific research programs. These programs, of paramount importance for national progress today, exist only as they revolve around the library, the coordinator of informational and research materials.

The library, as President Kennedy observed, is no longer the handmaiden to education, but is as important to education as classroom instruction. In all areas of education, from elementary school to the highest academic level, advanced educational methods forsake the textbook-oriented classroom and turn to the library as the center of instructional materials.

Libraries embrace the entire scope of human knowledge. As the supply of information increases—in science alone, each decade sees greater advancement than has been experienced in all of recorded history—so will libraries grow in significance and assume increasing importance in service to mankind.

Throughout the nation the expanding concept of library service is obvious. Public libraries, through regional development, are uniting cooperatively to meet the growing informational needs of people everywhere. Plans for new school buildings invariably include space for impressive library facilities, and older school buildings are being adapted to add instructional materials centers. College and university libraries are investigating and experimenting with data processing, and exploring cooperative methods of combining or eliminating detail and routine in order to devote more time to faculty research and student instructional needs.

The special library—in business, industry, government, and the professions—is growing at a phenomenal rate. All of this is obvious to anyone who observes the handsome new library buildings which are an integral part of urban renewal everywhere; the college campus, where the library is regularly the most impressive of the new buildings, located in the heart of the campus to indicate its function as central to the entire college program; the increasing number of computerized information centers around which industrial research now revolves. All of this reflects exciting development in the future, as well as the present, for libraries and librarianship.

The college graduate who seeks intellectual, educational, professional involvement in the dynamic world he faces should, in weighing career choices, consider the opportunities and advantages of librarianship. If his interests are in the direction of administration, research, education, information, or service, libraries offer fulfillment and excellent career opportunities.

The expansion of libraries, and the cultural trends and social forces which create a continually greater demand for library service, have seriously strained the professional resources of librarianship. The shortages and the growing vacancies have created a dilemma for libraries today.

At a time when more and more college graduates are entering the library profession—graduate library schools have doubled the number of graduates in the past five years—the cumulative needs of the library profession are much greater than the supply of fresh talent. This situation guarantees excellent placement and advancement opportunities to the bright, ambitious student who is prepared to devote a year of graduate study to obtain the master's degree in library science. Further study in doctoral programs is also available to the librarian today. However, the master's degree in library science provides full professional status for library careers.

The graduate curriculum in library science regularly requires concentated study in the various professional areas: library administration, reference and research, and technical processing (selection, acquisition and classification of library materials). The program includes study of the history of books, printing, libraries and library development. Through additional elective courses, the student is enabled to specialize in a selected area or aspect of librarianship, or to study in depth the service and administration of a particular type of library.

This, then, is a key to the future for the student who would associate himself professionally with his fellow man. The prospect for the librarian is an exciting one. He is involved in all of man's thoughts and activities and recorded knowledge. He is in the mainstream of cultural, social and educational change. Today's librarian is the man in the center.

## 31

## SERVICE FOR THE COMMUNITY

*By* EDWARD G. FREEHAFER

"Why didn't I think of that?" said a college classmate in mock envy when I told him I had decided to become a librarian. "What a soft life—go to work, stamp a few cards, spend the rest of the day reading in your ivory tower!"

He was only half joking. His impression of my chosen work was what he had seen in casual visits to look up a fact or borrow a book. To him, "librarian" meant the attendant behind the desk of a hushed reading room.

Like so many otherwise well-informed people of today, he had only the vaguest idea of the enormously varied duties, opportunities, and rewards that public library service offers. There is good reason. There have been custodians of the written and printed word ever since man began to record his knowledge, but librarianship as a modern profession is relatively quite new and has had to grow up very fast to keep pace with the phenomenal expansion of our libraries.

The first circulating library in this country was organized in 1731, in Philadelphia. It was more a club than a library since its use was restricted to its subscribers. As for a librarian—there wasn't one unless you count the member who volunteered to keep a list of borrowers, without pay. His name was Benjamin Franklin.

Not until 1833 was our first tax-supported, free circulating, public library opened. Little Peterborough, New Hampshire, made that important big stride.

The idea caught on. Free libraries, supported all or in part by public funds, came into being with almost explosive rapidity.

Today, we have more than 8,000 public library systems, not counting several thousand branch libraries. These vary in size from the New York Public Library with its 80 miles of shelves in the Central Building alone, and a staff of over 2,000, to county libraries that serve readers in isolated communities by bookmobile.

Not too long ago, a high school graduate could start as a page and eventually become a librarian, learning as he worked, usually for quite low wages. That is no longer the case.

As libraries grew, so did the need for qualified staffs to run them. Today, the title "trained librarian" ordinarily means one who has completed the five years of study at college or university level leading to a master's degree.

Having a job in a library does not necessarily require the individual to be a librarian. At least half of the staff of a large library has training in other fields. There are the clerical workers, the business machine operators, microfilm technicians, building maintenance workers, bookbinders, and scores of other specialists. As a general rule, you do not find the graduate librarian behind a charging desk. His time is spent in reference work, book selection, group discussion leadership, program planning, and a multitude of other specialized activities.

Salaries have kept pace with increased educational requirements, but the demand for librarians far exceeds the supply. This means that a qualified librarian can pick and choose when it comes to where he wishes to work and what sort of position he would like.

If you like the bustle and complexities of a big city, a large public library may be your goal. If you like to play an active part in a neighborhood, branch libraries of big systems or libraries in small towns will put you in close touch with your fellow citizens, their needs, their aspirations.

There has been a trend in recent years, given added impetus by federal legislation, toward cooperation among libraries. Regional systems of libraries are developing in most of the 50 states. Local financial support is aided or matched by state or federal funds to serve county and multi-county units. State-wide plans for service make the resources of the finest reference libraries available to the reader in the smallest town.

Marian, the Librarian, may have been able to run the memorable library of River City, Iowa, in Meredith Willson's *Music Man,* but the modern public library is a different proposition. The *Wall Street Journal* pointed out, in an article about modern libraries, that you can no longer say of the librarian, "Color her gray."

The director of a large system of libraries has a budget which may total millions of dollars, and responsibilities which compare with those of the chief officer of an industrial corporation. And as libraries increase in size, specialization increases. Positions develop for administration, business management, personnel and public relations. Book specialists for various age levels coordinate services throughout a system. Specially trained librarians provide service to the handicapped, reach out to the illiterate and under-educated. Audio-visual specialists administer film and record collections.

There is room for the subject specialist, too. The central library of a system is likely to have, as a minimum, half a million books divided into broad subject areas. A librarian with an interest or special training in a particular subject can find great rewards in giving aid in the use of materials in his field.

"Science is my hobby, but I don't want to be an engineer or technician," said a young man who came to me for career advice. "Is there any way I can concentrate on the sciences in library work?"

He could and did. He is now the head of a large technical collection, building a sound career and making a valuable contribution in the field of his keenest interest.

Many of us are appreciators of the arts and sciences without having the desire or the temperament to be creators or performers in them. There are few special interests from Art to Zoology that cannot be turned to account in a library.

Given people of all these various skills and backgrounds, what kind of an institution is today's public library? It is a source of intellectual energy in everyday life at all levels. No longer a quiet haven for a book-loving few, it has moved ahead in recent years in quality, breadth and depth of service.

Special subject collections are developed and shared by groups of libraries. Requests are relayed by teletype to speed up service. Photocopies are mailed to individual readers who need a short article or an illustration.

The great new world of electronics is appearing on the horizon. Computers are being used in acquistion procedures and record keeping. Electronic information storage, retrieval and transmission, while still presenting technical as well as financial problems, is being carefully explored in larger public library systems, in the great research libraries and in the special libraries of business and industrial companies.

The public library in this seventh decade of the twentieth century is a vital center for ideas. It has high standards. It deserves and demands the best, but in return it offers a position of influence and dignity in the community, a title of which anyone can be proud, and the knowledge that each day's work is a valuable contribution to education, amusement, solace or inspiration.

32

## SPECIALIZED FACT FINDING

*By* BILL M. WOODS

Aardvark to zymurgy; Maine to California; $7,000 to $25,000; industry and business to government, associations, and universities—such is the range and variety offered by a career in special librarianship.

What is special librarianship? Is it, as one guidance counselor declared recently, the best kept secret of the library profession? Special libraries are organized within business and industry, government agencies, trade and professional associations, museums, hospitals, and public and university libraries. They are reference and research libraries organized to meet the specialized needs of their parent organizations for accurate and up-to-date information. They differ in this respect from other types of libraries where the supplying of the physical book, periodical, or other material is likely to be the principal service.

Perhaps the who, what, and where of special libraries can best be answered by example. Fifty special librarians work for the International Business Machines Corporation in 26 libraries in the United States. (There are 11 more libraries outside the U.S. employing 20 special librarians.) Men, incidentally, head 11 of the 26 domestic libraries. At least nine more professional librarians work in various information and administrative capacities.

IBM as a decentralized corporation has a variety of research, engineering, and manufacturing divisions. In addition to technical libraries in advanced engineering, advanced basic science, and production, there are legal, business and training libraries. The first IBM library was founded in 1933 at Endicott, New York, while in late September, 1966, the 26th came into being at Cape Kennedy in Florida.

IBM's corporate Director of Information Retrieval and Library Services, Eugene B. Jackson, is a science graduate of Purdue; he studied engineering for a year at Texas Tech, and received two professional degrees in librarianship from the University of Illinois. Other IBM librarians have backgrounds in linguistics, mathematics, liberal arts, chemistry, journalism, business, and electrical engineering.

It's natural to expect IBM libraries to be using the latest developments in systems and hardware. One library, in the Advanced Systems Development Division in Los Gatos, California, has two of 36 terminals sharing real time on a laboratory computer. Routine library operations—acquisition of materials, processing, and circulating—are automated.

Other special libraries have found ways to make their work easier and efforts more efficient. Most—but not all—are small, and highly-trained professional manpower must not be wasted. A recent survey disclosed that 292 special libraries are now using and 353 are actively planning to use automated equipment.

Other large corporations in the *Fortune* "500" employ a large number of librarians—22 in Union Carbide, 36 in General Motors—as do advertising agencies, hospitals, newspapers and other publishers.

Time, Inc., for instance, has 109 persons (22 professional librarians) in its Editorial Reference Bureau headed by Peter Draz, who holds masters degrees both in history (Penn) and in library science (Western Reserve), and who came to Time after nine years experience with the *New York Times* and the Library of Congress.

Federal government agencies are principal employers of special librarians—some 3,400 librarians in more than 1,300 libraries. A recent U.S. Office of Education survey revealed that the 50 state governments maintain nearly 400 libraries in a variety of fields—history, agriculture, planning, public health, etc. There are more than 5,000 museums in the U.S. and several hundred have libraries.

There is a tremendous shortage of qualified personnel in all fields of librarianship, and this is particularly acute in special librarianship. There are equal opportunities for men and women.

Major libraries like those at Rand Corporation, Federal Reserve Bank of New York, Washington University School of Medicine, McGraw-Hill, Aerospace Corporation, UCLA Graduate School of Business Administration are headed by women.

Special librarianship also offers unique opportunities for qualified Negro librarians (major positions held by Negroes include the Federal Aviation Agency, Merck Sharp & Dohme, and Xerox).

Positions are open in all parts of the United States and Canada, and in other countries as well. There are some restrictions on mobility depending upon the choice of fields. For instance, most advertising libraries are in New York City; book, newspaper, and museum libraries are found generally in the large cities; technical research and development libraries are often located in suburban areas, with some in fairly remote areas such as the White Sands Missile Range in New Mexico.

The special librarian must be Everyman, knowing his subject as well as his average user; he must be an expert in the literature of the subject; he must know how to acquire, organize, and retrieve the information and documents of interest.

For this, the salaries are showing an encouraging annual upward trend for beginning positions—somewhere around $7,500 with several hundred dollars more for those persons with science training.

Average salaries are around $9,000-$10,000. Many special librarians, especially in science and technology, do, though, earn salaries several thousand dollars above that figure. The Placement Service of the Special Libraries Association regularly lists a number of positions in the $15,000-$25,000 range.

Every college student specializes in some subject or field whether it be archeology or Zuluology, or the more likely possibilities of art, business, chemistry, economics, engineering, geography, history, music, physics, or political science.

After studying some of these subjects for four years, the student may not always see just how his college major can really be used following graduation. It's a good bet, however, that special librarianship can make profitable use of such interest and competence.

# VI
# ADVERTISING

# THE IDEA BUSINESS

## By Dan Seymour

Advertising can spoil you for any other business there is. That's not a warning. It's an invitation. An invitation to what has to be one of the world's most exciting, important and rewarding businesses.

Advertising has the excitement of being more than just one business. It's radio, it's television, it's printing, it's packaging, photography, psychology, sales writing, research, art, fashion, finance, marketing, management and more.

Advertising is an important part—and often the most interesting part—of just about every other business. Whether it's peanuts or political candidates, every new firm, every new idea that's going to go anywhere has to be introduced to the public. And advertising does the honors.

And advertising is a rewarding business. Besides being among the highest-paying fields today, there are other rewards. The satisfaction of being able to open a magazine or switch on TV and see something you've worked on and know that millions of people are seeing it and being affected by it. The fun of working with some of the brightest, most creative and energetic people anywhere. The stimulation of being in a business that's one of the greatest sources of new ideas in our society.

Just what is the nature of this exciting, important and rewarding business? Where can you find it? How does it work? And how do you start a career in it?

You can find advertising in one of three places: the advertising department of a company or corporation, the advertising department of a radio or TV station, a newspaper or magazine, or in an advertising agency. Of these three, the advertising agency is really at the heart of the business. The agency is a separate business that offers to other businesses—its clients.

The client, of course, knows his product better than anyone else. The agency, on the other hand, knows the consumer. And the connection is made by means of advertisements. The agency creates, prepares and places advertisements.

How? In simplified form, the procedure goes something like this:

First the agency does a good deal of research into the product, its potential markets, its competition and any other pertinent subjects. Then the agency sits down with the client to plan the overall advertising strategy and budget.

Armed with research, a strategy and a budget, the agency then creates one or more advertising approaches—doing copy, layouts, radio and television scripts, whole campaigns—in rough form. These roughs are then presented to the client, discussed, perhaps changed, and eventually approved.

Once approved, the ads are prepared. That is, put into finished form by making and assembling photographs, drawings, engravings, films, tapes and anything else needed to make an ad suitable for presentation to the public.

While this is going on—and sometimes beforehand—space and time are bought in the appropriate media, so that, when the ads are finished they are delivered to these media ready to print or broadcast.

There, in an admittedly over-simplified form, is an outline of what an agency does. Now let's take a look at the career opportunities you can find there.

*The account executive* is a manager, liaison man and a salesman.

It's his job to draw together the desires of the client, the talents of the agency and the potentials of the media to make advertising work for the client.

But ads don't just come out of the air. They come from the creative people in the agency—starting with the writer.

Though some people call it the Word Business, I think it's more accurate to call Advertising the "Idea Business."

And *the writer* is the idea man.

Both client and agency look to him to uncover a unique point of view—often stated in a slogan of 10 words or less—that will bring about a sense of communication between product and consumer. A sense of communications so strong that you can see it in the sales curve.

The writer has to have an awareness that extends into all areas.

He has to know consumers—their needs, their dreams and their language—whether they're teenagers, board chairmen or housewives. He has to know the techniques of all the media because he will often see an ad or commercial in his mind before he commits it to paper, and he has to know whether such an idea is feasible to produce.

# ADVERTISING

And, of course, he has to understand his product or products. Inside and out. And the competition's product too, to the point where he may find a unique appeal in his product that no one—not even the client—knew was there.

He then must create a feeling, a mood, an aura, a reputation, a line, something that will make his ads—and through them, the product—stand apart from all others.

But finding the right words is only half the battle in the art of making printed advertising. The other half is finding the right pictures, the right "look" for a particular product. That's where *the art director* comes in.

The art director is himself an artist in a very special way. He sees to it that all the elements of an ad come together to make it most effective.

He has to know what's in style, what's being done and what's being overdone.

Once the client approves a rough layout, the art director has to direct the people who do the finished art for the ad—photography, line art, watercolor, everything. He's on the scene when pictures are shot. And he sees the artwork at every stage of production to be sure the colors and the look of it are exactly right.

For television, the art director usually begins his job by making what's known as a storyboard—a series of pictures representing the video portion of the commercial.

The TV art director often helps select the technique to be used—still photos, motion, stop-action, cartoons, etc. He contributes visual ideas and dreams up new special affects. He can become as much or as little involved in the production of the commercial as he likes, because his job often overlaps with that of the producer.

Here is an area that's emerged as one of the most highly complex and technical in the business.

The print *production man* causes the art and the copy to be turned into materials—printing plates, etc.—to produce the ad in magazines, newspapers, on billboards or wherever they're to be seen.

To do this, he must contract through various typographers, engravers and printers of all sorts. He sees to it that each ad gets the best possible quality in type and photographic reproduction. At the right price. And usually in one big hurry.

Indeed, many production people help their agency keep certain clients merely on the strength of their ability to produce ads quickly in a fast-moving, short-deadline business.

But the print production man, as well as the radio and television producers, would have nowhere to send the ads if it weren't for *the media man.*

The media man plans and does the buying of print space for ads and air time for commercials.

To do this, he has to know which of the more than 1,800 daily newspapers, 600 national magazines, 2,000 business magazines, 3,300 radio stations, 500 TV stations and untold outdoor posters and direct-mail lists will be the best ones to use for a particular ad for a particular client.

He has to be aware of everything—right down to the mood of a magazine, the psychological environment of a TV show, the editorial authority of a newspaper, and more.

And he has to be a pretty good horse trader, too, in order to make smart buys, get good position for his ads and still keep within his budget.

One of the media man's great strengths has to be his knowledge of how many people with how much purchasing power can be reached in any one medium or combination of media within a given time period. For this information, he depends a good deal on the various rating systems, audience research, readership studies—and often, his agency's research department.

*The researcher* works for everyone. Including the consumer.

Media people ask him to find out about public acceptance of various media. Marketing men ask him to find out the size and nature of potential markets. Creative people ask him to test ads or campaigns either before or while they're running.

Those are some of the possible careers you can find at an advertising agency. But how do you know where you might fit in?

Well, one way is to look at the direction your school career is taking right now.

If, for instance, you're always involved in student government or always getting to organize the class dance, then you're probably headed for work in the account executive area.

If you spend lots of time writing on the school paper or entering short-story contests, you'll find plenty of outlets for your creative urge as a copywriter.

Interest in the campus radio station or drama club can lead you into the commercial production area. If you're an artist you may want to get into art directing or package design. If you enjoy psychology or statistics, you may enjoy research or computer work, which has only begun to explore its potential in advertising.

These are, of course, all generalizations. And an actor may end up writing, a writer may be a very effective account exec, or an art student can produce TV commercials. There's no hard and fast rule.

There is, however, one bit of advice I can give undergraduates: don't come into the advertising business only half-educated.

So take as many different courses, look over as many different subjects, get into as many different activities, meet as many people and see as much of the world as you can. Spread your world to include everything from the Mamas and Papas to the Bach family, from Romulus and Remus to the Marx Brothers, Cybernetics, Ty Cobb, Machiavelli, McLuhan, Bogey, Tom Brown, the Cleveland Browns, Werner Von Braun. Everything.

Because the indications are that today—and tomorrow— the advertising business will be looking for people with a broad background and an acute awareness of everything that goes on around them.

These are the people who will embrace the business in its entirety. The people who will be up on everything that's new. In on every project they have time for. And out in front of everyone else.

They're the people who will write tomorrow's legends in advertising.

And who knows? You may be one of them.

## 34

## THE CREATIVE PEOPLE

### By Whit Hobbs

I have one son in graduate school, one in college, one about to be in college, and it isn't only their *bills* that give me pause these days, it's also their *questions*. They add up to something like this: Come now, old timer, what kind of a crazy, mixed-up, cut-throat, silly, superficial, rat race business are you in, anyway?

To which I answer: You there, behind those expensive, ivy-covered walls, knock it off. Don't bite the brands that feed you. This is the only job I've ever had, and it's the only job I ever want. I'm proud of my profession. It's a darn good way to make a darn good living. I thrive on it, because it's the most exciting, challenging, fast-moving, difficult, rutless business I know; a wonderfully happy business for itchy, unhappy people. You may not live to an extreme old age, but what you die of never turns out to be boredom.

To be good at advertising, you have to live in a very wide world. You have to know so much about so many things. You have to get deeply involved in *all* business. This doesn't appeal to everybody; but the people to whom it does appeal, they're the people who appeal to me. Advertising people are special people.

I can't think of another business in which there is anything like as high a percentage of lively, eager, curious, savvy, talented men and women. Swingers. All of them young, regardless of their age. You *have* to stay young in the advertising business, because every year our customers get younger. There are now more people in the U.S. under 25 than over 25—and one-third of the population is 15 and under. Advertising people work hard, they're conscientious, they're honest. You can't be anything else in this goldfishbowl business we're in without being shown up and run out of town.

Of course, advertising has its lunatic fringe, its double dealers, double martinis, double talk. Its pointed shoes and pointed heads. No business is without them. But they're unimportant.

What's important is that advertising today is more dynamic than it has ever been. And the really good creative people in it are more determined than they have ever been. Determined to get rid of the tired and the tasteless and the trite and do stuff that is *excellent*.

What's important, too, is that there is an enthusiastic audience out there, waiting for the best we have to give them. Believe it or not, people *like* advertising. They don't like all of it, of course, and obviously there is too much of it; *what they like is advertising that likes them*. Advertising that understands them, flatters them, informs them, helps them, amuses them, challenges them, saves them time and work and money, tries hard to be their friend. Please, they say, get rid of that White Knight on that white horse who keeps riding past my house and scaring the hell out of my kids. And please, won't somebody shut the kitchen window so that stupid dove won't keep flying in. And please, let's stop sloshing through all those clogged sinus passages. . . .

And so advertising is trying hard to please rather than to exasperate, and in doing just that, it is becoming the liveliest of the lively arts. The writing is tight and bright, the photography is superb, the music is exciting, the total effect is bold and compelling. Take all the ads out of your favorite magazine and you have taken out more than half of the fun and flair and finesse. Watch an evening of television and again and again you will see commercials that have more showmanship, more craftsmanship than the shows which surround them.

Where is this business going? It's going professional. The agency business is changing. Growing increasingly competitive, increasingly demanding, increasingly complex. As today's client grows more and more sophisticated, the client-agency relationship is changing. Today, the client finds himself with a choice. On the one hand, he can regard his agency as a group of specialists whom he employs to get their feet wet in his business and give him answers to certain specific problems. For example, answers in the creative area, recommendations in media.

Or, on the other hand, he can treat his agency as a full business partner. He can take his agency into his full confidence, and from his agency he can expect the full treatment. The full resources of every department of the agency brought to bear on his immediate and his long-range business. This is the way of the future. Being a great deal more than the name "advertising agency" encompasses. Being a total marketing partner. Total involvement. Knowing as much about his business as he does.

And so today's client is not only growing more sophisticated, he is also growing more demanding. He wants a helluva lot for his money.

He wants imagination and soundness and guts. He wants to hear what the agency really believes, not what they believe he wants to hear. He wants a selling idea for his product that is original, exclusive, appealing to the customer—that grows out of a selling strategy that he and the agency have developed for the product. He wants a brilliant execution of that selling idea that is fresh and compelling—and 100 per cent on strategy, on target.

Through it all, he wants sound, sensitive research. Solid answers. *Proof* that it will work. He wants advertising that is bold and exciting. And this is what the best clients are getting. Because bold, exciting creative people clamor to work this way. The best creative people want the highest, most professional standards, the most challenging challenge they can get.

If the agency is a full marketing partner, this means doing it the hard way. This doesn't mean going to the client with a pastry tray full of goodies (many of them only half-baked) and saying, "Here are some things we cooked up; do you see anything here you like?"

It means beginning with a selling strategy. A clear definition of the problem. A clear direction that emerges because all the data has been gathered and studied; the problem has been carefully thought through. And then sitting down and coming up with a creative solution that is dazzling *and* that hits the target dead center. *This* is what today's client is looking for. So is today's customer.

Now let's talk about you. Two questions: (1) Would advertising be good for you? (2) Would you be good for advertising?

If you are looking for challenge and excitement, this is where you'll find both. My end of the business, the creative end, is looking for bright, artistic, articulate, enthusiastic, young people. People who have a way with words, who are excited about ideas, who are keenly interested in other people, in what makes them tick and what makes them buy.

It used to be that an advertising agency was rigidly departmentalized. There was a Copy Department and an Art Department, with a wall between the two. There was a wall between people who worked in radio and TV and those who worked on ads for newspapers and magazines. There was a wall between those who did consumer ads and those who did trade ads. And there were other walls—between creative people and research and account management people. It was like the days when there used to be Departments of Army, Navy and Air Force with all the red tape and jealousies and duplication and nonsense.

Then advertising grew up. And so did the people in it. And the walls came down. Today, except in a few backward agencies, the trend is toward one Creative Department. And so an advertising writer, for example, is more versatile than he used to be. His job is more challenging because it has increased in scope.

And his job is more difficult than it used to be because every year the competition is keener and the customer is harder to sell and keep sold, harder to please, harder to intrigue.

Get one thing straight: this is a tremendously difficult job. In today's overcrowded world, with everyone shouting at once, it isn't easy to get through all the clutter and the clatter and be noticed and remembered. From the time a customer gets up in the morning until he (or, more likely, she) gives up at night, he/she has been bombarded by more than 1500 commercial messages. And so, doing good advertising is no longer good enough to stand out in the crowd. It has to be better than good.

Should you come and see us at the agencies? Yes, you should. The people in the advertising industry are looking for fresh creative talent. At Benton & Bowles, for example, we visit many of the leading campuses. We hire about half a dozen trainees a year in the Creative Department. We pick them very carefully. We pay them very well. We move them up (in responsibility and in money) as fast as they are able to move.

What should you bring with you when you come?

Bring things you're proud of. Writing you have done, for instance, whether it is close to advertising or not. We want to know that you can put the words down—and put the ideas down—in a fresh, interesting, orderly, compelling way.

Bring a good education.

Bring a good sense of humor.

Bring a keen interest in everything.

Bring a strong back.

Bring an insatiable curiosity.

Bring an honest conviction about advertising—that it is a dynamic, useful profession that you will be proud to be in. If you're a cynic or a smart aleck, please go somewhere else.

Bring taste and style. Both are hard to define, hard to describe, but you know without a description whether or not you have them. If you have 'em, bring 'em.

35

## THE PROSPECTS AHEAD

By Thomas B. Adams

While it is quite traditional to speak of the future of one's business in almost exclusively glowing terms, I instead want to survey some of the negative areas of advertising. I have done this because I'm convinced that no one is interested in entering a field that, ostrich like, pretends that all the problems have been solved.

We have problems, and I am covering two of our weightier ones with the hope that I may uncover a desire among you to jump in and help us to solve them.

But first, a word about future economics.

As our economy grows more complex, more and more new products will be developed and introduced. In the years to come such mass distribution techniques of the retailing revolution as self-service stores, vending machines, and one-stop shopping will be improved and expanded.

With the absolute necessity of producing more products to meet the needs of our future economy, advertising will play an increasingly essential part since unsold goods have no value.

Advertising, then, will remain an inextricable part of our economy's future. The volume of advertising must increase to move the mounting goods necessary to sustain a population increasing in number, affluence and leisure time.

To continue a healthy growth, advertising must attack some of its current problem areas in the immediate future. Although the basic product of advertising is communication, we have failed distinctly in communicating with certain segments of our society that are immensely important to us. One of these important segments is the academic world.

It is the people who comprise this world who so very often take a dim and voluble view of advertising and pass this attitude along to their students. I realize we will always have critics in the academic as well as other communities and probably should have, but I feel that everyone in advertising must do his best to communicate with and inform these critics so that the criticism may be at least realistic and constructive.

Advertising is the most visible element of our economic system. When critics of this system are looking for a target, advertising, whether or not it is the guilty party, is easy to attack.

Some of the truths which we must impart to the academic community in the future include the fact that advertising is not a group-minded, monolithic organization, close knit in a mutual vow to either annoy or entertain. This objective truth has a hard way to go to make headway against national comments aimed at such a conveniently visible target.

Advertising is simply a part of our economic system. And it is only a part. Advertising did not create our economic system, but it is now, for better or worse, absolutely indispensable to it. Advertising is not the economic force of this country. It is the accelerator of this economic force.

Our surveys indicate that most intellectuals are inclined to accept the fact that advertising is a beneficial factor in our economic system. Having made that concession, however, they criitcize the rate of consumption in this country as though production were a virtue and consumption a sin.

Yet, those who profess this belief cannot understand our economy where luxuries paradoxically have almost become the staples of this system. The part of the dollar required by the average family for essentials is 52c, and it is shrinking. In what some people refer to as the good old days, 94c out of every dollar was needed for essentials. It is obvious, then, that our burgeoning economy cannot be supported merely through the marketing of essentials.

Advertising must get these economic facts of life across to the intellectual community and, at the same time, communicate what disciplines we need to have them develop.

For where but from the intellgentisa does any society derive its systems and its mode of living. And advertising needs the addition of creative and individual personel who are in touch and avant garde.

It is the academic community that persists in accusing our society of becoming materialistic, without carrying the charge any further to pinpoint from where the materialism was derived. The charge actually falls right back from where it issues.

Materialistic behavior is that activity which is viewed as being purely mechanistic. Where but from a segment of the academic community, the psychologists, have we arrived at this view?

In reviewing the psychologists' field of study since the earlier part of this century, we discover that we've been sold an over-simplified, materialistic, mechanical concept of the human phenomenon made up of stimulus, organism and response—S.O.R. This approach reduces the human being to the level of one of Pavlov's dogs, capable of no more than responding mechanically to stimuli through conditioning.

In an intellectual climate where the study of human behavior is so thoroughly limited, the ridiculous charge that advertising sells unneeded products to unwilling consumers against their desires gains credence. If we recognize that the human conscious mind is possessed of a free will, these charges appear absurd.

It is not in my area to either define or dictate what psychology should be. If the psychologist chooses to define his science in the materialistic sense, however, then his discipline offers only a limited mechanical value for our business. We will then have to find whoever can do the work and support their efforts so that they can contribute to our business by developing a true understanding of it in terms of the content, meaning, and effectiveness of advertising to the human mind. This will be one of the most important tasks in the future of advertising.

Advertisers are asking their agencies more often and more precisely to account for the effectiveness of the advertising we are doing. In the future this trend will increase rather than diminish.

We cannot wait, though, until the academic world either develops a new discipline or changes direction in an existing one before we vastly improve our communications with another important audience, the federal government.

We know that the work of our Advertising Council has won us the respect of many people in Washington. We have demonstrated our concern for matters of public interest. We have mobilized hundreds of millions of dollars in advertising and talent and resources in support of government projects. We have made Smokey the most famous bear of all time, and, among other Washington activities, we have helped the U.S. Office of Education. And we have done these things, and more, without asking or expecting anything in return. Moreover, we intend to continue on this course.

Many of those in Washington applauding the efforts of the Council, however, are also questioning the role of advertising in our economy. In the future, advertising is going to have to reevaluate its approach to Washington for we simply aren't communicating effectively with the government.

The worn out and defeating attitude that business, advertising included, has aodpted in the past, that the government is on one side of the fence and we are on the other, must be discarded completely in the next 10 to 15 years.

It is important that people in advertising realize that it is possible to be an influence in government. My observations are that the government will listen to us, if we will only talk to them. There are people in Congress and in the regulatory agencies who indicate that they are anxious for help.

If we in advertising will uncoil our legs, climb out of our chairs, and go and see people in government, whether they be in Washington, or in our individual states or in our cities, we can be heard. And we can be an influence on those issues that affect advertising.

Last year after a detailed study, the American Association of Advertising Agencies opened an office in Washington, and this action was applauded by most of the advertising agency membership. Although the office at this point holds no official title, it could readily be called the Office of Advertising Information. It is not intended as a defensive mechanism nor one that has a pert secretary waiting for the telephone to ring. I understand this office is a digging, running offensive operation searching out influential voices in Congress and in the regulatory agencies to make sure that the advertising industry is understood in detail before legislative thinking crystallizes on a solution to a particular problem.

Personally, I am delighted that these first steps have been taken and that our business has a corrector of misinformation functioning in Washington.

Not only has advertising the duty and the need to help and inform the federal government, it has that same duty and need to the local state and city governments where our agencies' various headquarters, divisions and branch offices are located. Last year in cooperation with Governor Romney's office in Michigan, my agency wrote and produced a series of television documentaries on water pollution, crime and education.

I don't know whether what we did will result in legislation in the state, but certainly it has resulted in greater public awareness of problems very real in Michigan and throughout our country. And perhaps we have contributed to a new resolve by all levels of government, and the people, to begin searching for solutions to these national problems.

This example represents only the beginning of what we and all other advertising agencies must do in the future. In our role as communications experts we must aid all branches of our government in defining and solving problems. This is by no means sheer altruism, since these problems will give us an opportunity to learn more of governmental functions while, at the same time, government will be given a far better view of us than would otherwise be possible.

# THE WAY YOU SAY IT

## By William Bernbach

In the word business, it's not just what you say that stirs people. It's the way that you say it.

The idea that war is absurd has been made in many forgettable books. But "Catch-22" immortalized the absurdity of war. The difference between the forgettable and the immortal is artistry. That's true in advertising, too. You can say the right thing about a product and nobody will listen. You've got to say it in such a way that people will feel it in their gut. Because if they don't feel it, nothing will happen.

Nothing is what happens 85 percent of the time. Eighty-five percent of all ads are ignored by the American public. Not hated, not scorned, just ignored. That's what an industry study, commissioned by the American Association of Advertising Agencies, showed.

But why should your ad be noticed? The consumer doesn't buy a publication to read the ads, nor tune in radio or TV for the commercials. Moreover, he is confronted daily with a world of violence, with world-shaking events, history-making news. With this deafening roar of frightening conflict beating about his ears, how do we expect him to hear our advertising story? And if we do pierce this wall of violence, how do we get through the second wall, an almost impenetrable wall of competition crying its wares?

You can eventually make some kind of impression, of course, with a tremendous advertising budget and constant repetition. But what a waste. You can instead use the far more practical weapon of artistry—artistry that tells the story of the product or service in memorable, convincing fashion; that makes it stand out from the throng of similar competitive products or services.

Now if you believe, as I do, that advertising is an art, not a science, there is obviously nothing either to ask or say about rules and formulas for writing advertising copy. Rules are what the artist breaks; the memorable never emerged from a formula.

But *principles* are another matter, and I'd like to tell you about some we have at our agency. You'll forgive me if I use our own work to illustrate these principles. I do it because I know what the motivations were, and I can give you facts and figures.

1. *Impressions outweigh numbers.* Nobody counts the number of ads you run; they just remember the impression you make. Ohrbach's, a store noted for its low prices, does one-fortieth the amount of advertising that Macy's does in New York City. Yet in some surveys, when people are asked "Who does the greatest amount of department store advertising?" Ohrbach's comes out first with Macy's, and all the other stores follow.

What could be more practical to the businessman than having advertising that does many times the job of the competition?

Low prices are not associated with high fashion, yet Orbach's sells more Paris copies than any store in America. When *Life* magazine runs a story on Paris imports, the story is built around Ohrbach's. That's what can happen when a company's advertising stops people, touches them, and persuades them.

2. *Do the right ad at the right time.* There is no such thing as a good or bad ad in isolation. What is good at one moment is bad at another.

The worst ads in the world are those that say "Everybody's talking about (blank's) so-and-so" when nobody's talking about it. You fool no one.

You must earn your respect from the American consumer. You can't just jump in and say, "Look at me, "I'm great." You have to earn it by giving the consumer facts and figures.

I remember our first ad for Levy's bread—a bread firmer than most. You know the habit many people have of squeezing a loaf of bread before they buy it. We said, "Are you buying a bed or bread?" We went on to tell them that when you put the proper things into a bread it isn't as soft as you'd like it to be but it's better for you. We ran that kind of advertising for about a year. The sales rose, Levy's was fast becoming the best selling rye bread in New York.

The bread wasn't always called Levy's real Jewish Rye. It was called Levy's Real Rye. I had the feeling we should call it Real Jewish Rye, but Mr. Ruben, who runs the company, was a little worried. "I mean, after all, why look for trouble?" he said. "I'm sure a lot of people feel anti-Semitic—why should we rub it in?" I said. "What do you think people will think you are with the name Levy?" We put it in, and it was wonderful. Jewish Rye means a certain kind of rye. It informs the public. For my money, the best ad in the world is an ad that informs the public. Memorably.

When we got the El Al account, it was a small airline, almost unheard of. The company had just bought two Britannia jet props, which were two hours faster across the Atlantic Ocean than the ordinary props running at that time. We could have run an ad that said "Two hours faster across the Atlantic"—a perfectly good ad. Nothing wrong with it, except that we couldn't afford just to have a good ad. We had to make one ad do the work of ten. So we ran an ad that said: Starting Dec. 23 the Atlantic will be 20% smaller."

The morning after the ad appeared, there was a rush of phone calls for reservations. El Al had to install two new telephone trunk lines to take the orders.

3. *The innovator gets the credit.* While working on the El Al account, we found out that the greatest source of income to an airline is the travel agency. At the time no one in the business had done any kind of advertising on the travel agent. The average person wasn't aware of the kind of service the travel agent gives, and that it is the carrier or the hotel who pays for the service rather than the traveler. And so we practiced that sensible idea of serving the consumer. We ran an El Al ad entitled "Just What Does A Travel Agent Do For You?"

The American Express Company put the ad in their windows around the world, and perhaps they felt kindly toward El Al because we had done them a good turn. Since then, many airlines have followed with similar ads. But the guy who does it first gets the credit. The copies only remind people of the first ad they saw.

Just one more El Al story. The jets came, and we no longer were faster across the Atlantic. As a matter of fact, we were slower. But in those early days the gas tanks in the jets were not as big as in the Britannia jet props. Most of the jets had to refuel at Goose Bay, Labrador, and Gander. We didn't. So we quickly ran an ad that said "No Goose, no Gander." In a year when we were slower than most of our competition, there were tremendous gains in passenger fares.

4. *Create personality.* One of the things we must do in our advertising for our client is to create a personality, an individuality. Without that, whether you're a person or a department store or an airline or any other business, you're not going to make it.

We had noticed a graphic similarity among most airline ads. When American Airlines gave us their account, we created a look that was like no competitor's. This particular ad was the most-noted and best-read ad in *Time* magazine where we ran it—not just among airplane ads but of all the ads in the publication.

We did the same kind of thing for Colombian coffee. We created a character named Juan Valdez.

Colombian coffee has risen from a virtually unknown name in coffee to an almost universally recognized name. Up to the launching of our campaign, the public was buying the roaster's name, and had no awareness of whether Colombian coffee was used. Today there are, throughout the country, about 70 brands of 100 percent Colombian coffee. None of them existed before. When you survey the American public, they know about Columbian coffee and they know that is perhaps a superior product. Juan Valdez has become a real personality. They tell me they're thinking of putting him on a stamp of Colombia.

5. *Get your advertising believed.* The metabolism of the world has changed. The consumer is confronted by so much today, he doesn't have time to analyze or investigate. He doesn't know whom to believe.

Here is an ad for a company called Utica Club Beer.

When we got the account of Utica Club Beer, I talked with the man who owns the brewery, and asked him to tell us about his company. He was, we quickly learned, a bitter man. He said, "I don't know what to tell you. We have one of the great breweries in America. We have the best malt, the best hops, we have the latest equipment that my father brought over from Germany. But sometimes I wonder if it pays to make beer this way. People want a gimmick."

We ran our ad with the headline "I sometimes wonder if it pays to make beer this way." Here was obviously an angry, bitter man. We didn't use a slick headline that said, "Buy me, I'm the best," or "Why I'm eight ways better than my competition." Here was an angry man, and, because he was angry and human, people believed him.

We signed the ad with his name. Walter J. Matt. We went into the files and got pictures of his father and his father's colleagues, all authentic pictures. The ad ran. And literally by the thousands, letters poured in saying, "Please, Mr. Matt, don't go out of business. America needs honest businessmen like you." That kind of believability wouldn't have been achieved with slickness.

6. *Ads make impressions before they are looked at and read.* If somebody walked into the room you're in at this minute, you'd get an immediate feeling about him, even before he spoke. The same thing happens with an ad. You turn a page and, before you really compre-

hend it, there's a feeling. There's a vibration. That vibration, in our opinion, is a very important thing. If it's the wrong vibration for what you want to convey, what follows is going to fight it—an uphill battle against the original impression you made.

For example, Polaroid had been running ads that were crowded, reverse type, with arrows, and unattractive pictures. The page said, Cheap, a Novelty. The price said Expensive ( at that time, $100). Those two things don't go together.

Well, we changed it immediately.

We were selling pictures, so we showed pictures. We didn't have a logo. Yet, almost invariably, we were one or two in "seen-associated" *Life* readership tests.

This business of having to show a big logo can get you into trouble. Suppose you have a product whose image you want to change. People associate names with their established ideas of the name. When the name Robert is mentioned, and you know a man named Robert, you get a certain picture in your mind of a certain kind of person. You know all about him. The same thing happens on a page. You turn that page, you see a big name, you say, "I know all about it," and away you go.

Now suppose what you think about it is not what I want you to think about it? The only way out of that, in our opinion, is to present a very exciting thought and intrigue the person into the ad with that thought. Then gradually lead him to your product name and give him a new reason for remembering your name. This is the kind of thing that doesn't lose you any sponsor identification at all. In our experience, it makes it greater.

7. *Don't waste the reader's time.* It is one thing to get attention, but getting attention is not the total answer. You can get attention and really make people resent you if you do it with an unrelated gimmick. They won't like you for that. The thing to do is to have the very thing that gets attention stem from your product and convey the advantage you want to convey.

When we got part of the Clairol account we were told that we might have to show 12 women's heads in the ad. The product comes in 12 shades, and each one of them is important. Well, we could have shown 12 heads, and it would have been all right, but I don't think it would have been exciting. Instead, we looked for a devise that would draw attention and, at the same time, convey the advantages. We ran an ad that showed the most eye-appealing portions of 12 heads. We achieved economy and integration, getting attention and selling in one stroke.

8. *Make it memorable.* Not long ago we ran a Volkswagen ad with the word "Lemon" directly underneath a photo of the car. What we were talking about, as we explained in accompanying copy, was the inspection system at Volkswagen. One of the inspectors looked at the VW with a magnifying glass, and he sent it back to be repainted. He saw a scratch you couldn't see with your naked eye, yet he sent it back. We could have said, very easily, "We have the best inspection system in the world." But that's saying the right thing and getting no place—the same old unbelievable, boring story.

9. *The product must be good.* This principle is more important than any other, even more than believability, but it has more to do with the company than with us.

Seagram's owns Calvert whiskey. Calvert had gone down in sales to a point where the company was concerned. Mr. Edgar Bronfman asked me if we could work together on the problem. We got an idea, which was to introduce "soft" whiskey.

If we had run this ad with the whiskey they had, it would have been a complete flop. Calvert was a good whiskey but not a soft whiskey. Memorable advertising just makes a mis-represented product fail faster.

Mr. Bronfman—and I can't pay enough tribute to him—spent over $8 million calling in every single bottle of Calvert out on the market, making a new bottle, and putting a new whiskey into that bottle. When we launched this campaign, we had a great soft whiskey behind it. When people tasted the whiskey, they said, "That advertisement is right." The advertising didn't make the product work; the product made the advertising work.

Our Avis campaign was also conceived to make the product better. We took this campaign around to all the people who work at Avis—to car washers, mechanics, the girls behind the counter—and said, "Look, we're going to promise the American public that we're going to give them a cleaner car, a better-serviced car, and we need you. Never did any company depend on its employees as much as we are depending on you." And these people swelled with pride, they went to work, and we did have better service. Not perfect, but better. The result was that Hertz began to make theirs better, because they felt the competition. The beneficiary of this kind of advertising is the consumer, because he gets a better product.

Another point on Avis. Somebody in our shop insisted that we re-

# ADVERTISING

search the campaign. The research came back and said. Don't run it. People had said, "If you're only No. 2, you're not No. 1. And if you're not No. 1, you're not the best."

The company was in the red before this campaign started. A year later it was in the black for $1¼ million. We would have lost this campaign had we taken the research at face value. This is one of the big problems with research; it tends to keep you from thinking. It tends to make you feel you have the answer. You don't have the answer until you sweat over that research and you use your own judgment.

The theme of this campaign is not that we're No. 2. The theme is that we try harder. This is what the research didn't bring out. We got believability by telling people we're No. 2 but we'd like to be No. 1. People believe that somebody on the make is going to try hard, and that's why this campaign was a success.

These are our principles. What they add up to is that the idea must convey memorably (and because it is memorable, it must be fresh and original) the advantage of our product. If breaking every rule in the world is going to achieve that, we want those rules broken. Because unless our advertising moves people, we're not going to get anyplace.

## FACT, FICTION AND MONEY

### By JERRY FIELDS

One of the most paradoxical situations existing in our business community today is the ineffectiveness of the communications industry to deliver its own message to the young men and women it hopes to recruit for jobs in advertising, marketing and public relations.

To paraphrase the old song "Don't Put Your Daughter on The Stage Mrs. Worthington" many mothers now bemoan their fate if their sons embark on a career in the not quite legitimate field of advertising. Unfortunately many parents have formed their impression of the advertising business from the same source. These sources have been bad movies, equally bad novels, and even worse television shows. A best-selling novel like Kazan's *The Arrangement*, paints a picture of life on Madison Avenue that couldn't be further from the truth. Equally bad image-makers are movies like "The Man in The Grey Flannel Suit," "The Hucksters," "Mr. Blanding Builds His Dream House," just to mention a few in which the main character was an ad man and a fool, buffoon, cheat or scoundrel. It seems that in almost every script that is written in which the main character has to be involved in a business of some kind, or where the business itself is part of the plot, it's inevitably the advertising business. It's no wonder that in the eyes of a significant percentage of our business community ad men are considered to be not quite legit, maybe a cut or so above people in show business. Why don't authors who need a business or career man as part of their story, have them be less-than-honest insurance acturians, crafty accountants, shoddy architects or scheming automobile or food distributors? Is it because people are fascinated by the people in advertising? Is it that people don't want to hear about people plying prosaic trades but want to enjoy an involvement with the more interesting and colorful people in our economy? The fact of the matter is that people in advertising are more interesting, more colorful, more innovating, more amusing, than people in other professions. Advertising also has more than its share of playboys, sychopants, and professional dilettantes. But the business is getting tougher and tougher each year and the demands on its practitioners make it harder and harder for the deadline-obsessed, mortgage burdened, family oriented ad man to make the scene at all the mad Madison Avenue orgies to which he is constantly being invited.

Let's take a real honest look at the advertising and communications business through our eyes. For the past twenty years we have headed up the largest personnel recruitment company in the world specializing in the advertising and marketing fields. We have been responsible for placing thousands of men and women in jobs at all levels and have wet-nursed many of them from job to job, watching their salaries esculate from five to fifty thousand dollars in less time than it could in any other industry with the exception of Hollywood. Our point of view is a cold, hard pragmatic one. We and the other members of our staff earn our living by finding jobs for people in advertising so we can't afford to take an academic or theoretical view of the advertising business and the job market. We have to know what works because our livelihood depends on it.

Let's start off by saying that there is no business in our entire economy in which a talented young man or woman can make it as big and as fast as he can on Madison Avenue. There's a reason for this. One brilliant marketing plan, one idea for a new product, one great TV commercial or concept can result in a company making millions of dollars in the sale of a product or brand. No one working in the more prosaic area of our economy, other than technicians and research scientists have the opportunity for the kind of explosive breakthroughs as there are in the advertising business.

Many changes have taken place on Madison Avenue in the past fifteen years. Gone are the days when the scions of rich families went straight to Madison Avenue from their Ivy League campuses and joined the advertising fraternity. The old school tie, fraternity concept is dead and gone. It was killed by the intensity of competition and the inability of advertising management to enjoy the luxury of hiring old school chums. The track on Madison Avenue today is a fast one and creative and marketing skills are more in demand than good school and family references. However, in the areas of marketing and account management, an M.A. in Business Administration still carries a lot of weight.

What this all adds up to is that by far the larger percentage of the college students today have a completely warped idea of what really goes on in the advertising business. This false picture of the advertising business coupled with an emerging generation that looks at business with much misgivings makes the task of the advertising recruiter a difficult one. In part, a good deal of the blame for this distorted image can be laid at the door of the school faculty who themselves have really little knowledge of the ad business. More than likely, their antipathy towards advertising was indoctrinated in them when they were undergraduates.

If you don't draw or write and want to carve out a career in advertising then you should know something about what goes on in the advertising and marketing departments of companies and in ad agencies. Advertising is one of the most specialized areas in our economy. When an applicant is applying for a job through our company and tells us he is looking for "something in advertising" we know he has not done his homework. The fields of media, research, production, marketing, and sales promotion are just a few of the areas in which a young college graduate can get his start in advertising. Of course if you write or draw your task is infinitely easier. Copy and art people are king on Madison Avenue and staggering five figure salaries are being paid to young men, many of them not yet thirty, who can do creatively innovating things with words and pictures.

The problems of copy and art people in getting their start are far fewer than the man without either of these two skills. We instruct these young people in how to prepare copy or art portfolios that are mostly original concepts or reworking of ads that have already run. We refer to these samples as speculative portfolios—ads prepared as an exercise in what the individual can do with a creative assignment. In other words our answer to those people who complain that no one will hire them without experience and "how do we get this experience" is to make the experience.

The advertising business is hungry for talent of all kinds, and offers a world of stimulation and handsome monetary rewards. Any takers?

# 38

# THE ACCOUNT EXECUTIVE'S RESPONSIBILITIES

## By Tom Dillon

It would be a good deal easier to describe the function of an advertising agency account executive were it not for the unfortunate circumstance of his widespread appearance in stage, screen and popular fiction. As the fiction writers' darling, he has tended to replace the tough-talking reporter with snap-brim hat on the back of his head who, in an earlier cliche, picked up the phone and peremptorily ordered his city editor to hold the presses.

As is well known to all, the upbeat fictional account executive starts out as a very young and vastly overpaid young man who looks like Rock Hudson. His clients are pompous idiots who seek to thrust a breakfast food called "poopsie" on the unsuspecting public. His rich, but terrified, employer lets him spend most of his working day racing about Manahattan in a sports car with a beautiful girl photographer who is the estranged daughter of the client. At the end of a series of mad escapades, our account executive captivates the idiot client with the slogan "Love that Poopsie," and all kinds of good things happen.

On the downbeat side, the fictional account executive becomes enmeshed in the agency business by base motives of material gain. Relegated to living in the split-level ghetto of rural Connecticut, he and his wife eke out a drab life of heavy drinking, sexual immorality and intellectual stagnation. They are forced into this mold by the ruthless corporate compulsion to "conform." He moves through the business day in lockstep, wearing the agency's standard hat, coat, tie and cuff links.

But he is not safe in rigid conformity. For he is in the "jungle." All about him is malice and envy. Other men make "power moves" and he is crushed helplessly. He is torn between his own moral sense and the sinister pressures that drive him to mulct the innocent public. In a final confrontation with the forces of evil and stupidity, he breaks his shackles and returns, head high, to the cloistered halls of academic freedom and other good things.

Whether real life prototypes of these fictional account executives have ever existed, I do not know. I have not encountered them during my first thirty years in the advertising business. Perhaps I have led a sheltered life.

Any explanation of what a real account executive does in an advertising agency depends on an understanding of the key functions of the agency itself—the preparation of effective copy and the selection of the most effective media.

In order to do this the agency must:

(1) Know the product—from raw material down through manufacturing to the methods of its distribution through the channels of trade to the consumer.

(2) Know the consumer, what kind of person he is, where he lives, how he acts.

(3) Know the consumer's problems in the choice of products.

(4) Produce advertising copy that answers those problems in a way that gets the attention of the consumer in the midst of the thousands of messages being directed to him every day.

(5) Place this copy in time or space which most efficiently reaches the target consumer.

This apparently simple task requires a surprising amount of technological knowledge, and in order to bring this to bear, even a moderate-size agency is usually organized into specialized departments—marketing, research, media, copy, art, television and print production, and finally accounting.

And what does the account executive do about all this?

Inside the agency, his job is to manage the coordination of all of these specialized operations on behalf of his client.

For every account which an agency services, there is an account executive who heads a group of specialists from each of the departments. While each member reports to his department head in respect to his function, he also reports to the account executive in terms of specification of the work that is to be done for the client.

Outside of the agency's offices, the account executive plays another role. He is the principal bridge of communication between the agency and its client. On the client side of the bridge there is usually another large departmentalized industrial organization. He may have dozens of individuals from whom he must seek information and obtain approvals. Here again, the client organization is apt to be one of specialists, relatively few of them in the field of advertising.

There are very few analogies to the account executive's job in

# ADVERTISING

other businesses. He exists, as it were, in two worlds—the advertising world and the industrial world. His job is coordinating them in such a way that there is a smooth, effective relationship. This is not rendered easier by the fact that many of the specialists on both sides of this equation do not speak the same language. Industry language is heavily loaded with number concepts—dollars, quotas, shipments, return on investment, share of market. Copywriters and artists speak a language of abstract ideas, design, motivations and intuitions.

What kind of man does it take to be a good account executive?

A list of required homely virtues could be taken from the Boy Scout Handbook. It is, for example, an unprofitable occupation for a thief because nothing passes through his hands that is worth stealing. It is a bad place for a liar because one is too easily trapped. Indeed, the job is like working in a goldfish bowl. If you have anything to hide you have a severe problem.

Among successful account executives there are certain predictable human traits.

Perhaps the most noticeable is that they are highly self-motivated. Most of their work is done without close supervision. The standards of their performance are more likely to be set by inner drive than by outer pressure. They like people and people like them. They are good listeners and effective talkers. Inside and outside the agency they get people to do things for them because people want to do things for them. Authoritarian types are rarely successful.

They have perspective about time. They have the capacity to plan months ahead without losing track of the day-to-day flow of communication.

They are capable of organizing not only broad strategies, but of attending to a mass of detail. They have a proofreader's eye for mistakes, a wholesome respect for dates and a keen eye on the value of a dollar.

They have unusual intellectual curiosity. They absorb enormous amounts of information about their client's business and about the technology of advertising. Like a band leader, they do not necessarily know how to play each instrument better than the individual musicians, but they must know enough to communicate meaningfully with dozens of specialized talents.

They usually have a facility in writing English and public speaking.

What are the rewards of an account executive?

Most successful account executives seem to enjoy considerable psychological reward for their work. They sceem to feel it offers a wider variety of experience than most business occupations. They find their problems more stimulating than depressing. They seem to get satisfaction out of demonstrating their skills in organizing and directing a highly complex communications system.

In terms of a lifetime career, the successful account executive is usually very well paid by any industrial standards. This does not reflect the extravagance of advertising agencies, but rather the perennial shortage of people who can perform the account executive's function. It also reflects the fact that industrial firms tend to raid the ranks of agency account executives for marketing executive positions. Demand simply exceeds supply.

Perhaps the most attractive aspect for younger men is that an account executive can get recognition in pay and position at a relatively early age. Seniority and age do not stand in the way of a man who can perform the job.

In some agencies, there is also the incentive that the account executive can achieve ownership in part of the business, and there is a plainly marked path to agency management.

As a career opportunity, there are also negative aspects. So far no battery of psychological tests or analysis of educational backgrounds has been of much value in predicting whether a man will make a good account executive. It takes perhaps three years of on-the-job training before these talents become evident and a high percentage of prospects do not qualify.

During this period the advertising agency is investing its own money in an apprenticeship from which it receives comparatively little benefit. Often, if the man succeeds, he will take a position elsewhere and this investment is lost. This results in relatively few training positions and relatively low starting salaries. Both the agency and the man are gambling on the prospect that he is one of those rare individuals who have the necessary characteristics of becoming a crack account man.

There is also considerable difference of opinion as to whether it is wise to seek an account executive job as the first one after graduation. Many advertising executives think that it is more valuable in the long run to spend a couple of years in some marketing function for an industrial company. Others feel that it makes sense to have experience as a copywriter or a media man. Successful account executives have followed all of these routes.

Nor is there unanimity about whether one should start with a small agency or a large one. The small agency, or agency branch office, tends to broaden responsibilities of the account man and perhaps helps develop a better over-all perspective. The small agency, on the other hand, usually has a much lower pay scale and does not offer the exposure to the highly sophisticated personnel and techniques of the large agencies.

Being an account man is not everyone's cup of tea. Some of the apprenticeship is tedious. The hours may be irregular and long. There may be much travel away from home. Getting the cooperation of dozens of people may tax your powers of tact and imperturbability.

Carefully laid plans have a way of collapsing in a hopeless mess. Clients may be testy, copywriters outraged, networks intractable, agency management dour and your wife unsympathetic.

It is not everybody's job. But there are some of us who love it.

## THE PUBLIC RELATIONS SIDE

*By* BERT C. GOSS

Call it sad, call it funny, but it's better than even money that there's some beleaguered public relations man somewhere patiently trying to explain to somebody that he isn't really in the advertising business.

If I had a dime for every time a public relations man has been catalogued as "one of those advertising people," I could surely have amassed a tidy sum. I long ago resolved not to try to explain the differences to these well-meaning but uninformed inquisitors, preferring instead to let them think of public relations the way they think of a woman—something not to be understood but to be loved.

But as more and more businesses begin to recognize the value of public relations and more and more young people look to public relations as a career, it is important, I believe, to set the record straight.

What, then, is the difference between public relations and advertising? And why does the public look upon the professions with a sort of Damon and Pythias association?

One of the best definitions of advertising and advertisers that I've ever come across is contained in Walter Taplin's book, *Advertising— A New Approach*. "Advertisers," Mr. Taplin points out, "are constantly trying to discover what people want, or to guess what they want; to suggest new wants, or even to persuade people that they want things when they don't really want them at all."

Public relations, on the other hand, aims to inform in that it counsels and advises clients on public attitudes and represents them before the bar of public opinion; indeed, public relations, by definition, bears more of a family resemblance to journalism and teaching than to advertising.

While advertising may inform to the extent that consumers are made aware of a product or people become familiar with an idea through paid copy or television, public relations—always keeping in mind that what counts most are *sound* policies—may decide yes or no on the need to communicate at all. If communications are considered necessary, then an appropriate medium is selected to reach the particular audience.

Still, most people fail to disassociate one from the other. I think the basic reason for this is that people are considerably more familiar with advertising. They see advertising doing its job every day—on television and in the newspapers. It is a profession that is easily identifiable.

But most people cannot identify public relations quite so easily. They will speak of a company having a "good policy," but rarely realize that this policy most likely was born out of a well-thought-out public relations program. A business executive will deliver a speech that is well-received, but how many will recognize that a public relations man contributed suggestions that made its points more newsworthy and more acceptable to the public?

If there is a common denominator for both public relations and advertising, it is the effective use of communications. Both pursuits demand professional expression in language and pictures, and both find their ultimate outlets in the press, periodicals, radio and television. But it must be stressed that these points of similarily do not make public relations and advertising alike. Sandy Koufax and Johnny Unitas both use their arms to throw a ball but no real fan would confuse one sport with the other.

Inevitably young people ask about the type of career they can look forward to in public relations. I can only speak for myself, but I think the field is one of the most rewarding in the business world.

I have been a public relations man for 25 years. I was a newspaperman and editor for eight years before that. During these past 25 years, the scope and variety of my work has been such that it would do credit to any post-graduate college course. Certainly, you get out of a job whatever you put into it, but the opportunities that exist today in public relations, both financial and otherwise, are extensive.

It might be a good idea at this juncture to make one very important point. Don't plan on a career in public relations if you're looking for a job with rocking chair comfort. I know that many people still retain jaundiced views of what public relations men do. People imagine that we patronize the finer restaurants daily while spending most of our time either on the golf course or in a box seat at Yankee Stadium. It isn't so.

This attitude is undoubtedly manifested in the glamor and romance of press agentry which is as far removed from public relations as billiards is from bowling. It is not unusual for our account executives to work well into the night, poring over voluminous reports and tedious financial statements. If there is any glamor or romance attached to this kind of work, it comes from the effort to make dull and complicated material interesting and clear.

Beginning with the truism that corporations and industries retain public relations counsel to deal primarily with relationships with their various publics and the promotion of their products and services, it is quite obvious that you will encounter the problems that have caused them to seek outside advice and assistance. Here are some examples:

- A corporation seeks to merge.
- A corporation faces indictment for violation of antitrust laws.
- A corporation is confronted by union demands.
- A corporation has been losing vital personnel and must recruit more.
- A corporation chief executive is subpoenaed by an investigating committee.
- A company is attacked by politicians or newspapers because it allegedly causes air or water pollution.
- A corporation's chief product is being criticized by customers, doctors, health officials and others.

Solving problems such as these requires the application of a particular type of public relations philosophy. John W. Hill, founder of our company, puts it simply:

"When corporation policy is sound, it serves the community interest and is deserving of the support of public opinion. But this is not to say that it will get this support merely because it deserves it. The people must be informed. Lacking correct information, they may withhold their support. This is a job for public relations."

Going further he states . . .

"The corporation position must not only be explained in economic terms, but also be socially validated by references to yardsticks or principles that are esteemed and respected at every level of the American culture. The greater the objectives being sought, the greater the importance of justifying them in terms of their value to the whole American public.

"Those who would deal with public opinion must do so with all the understanding, intelligence and skill of which they are capable. Those of us who have spent many years in public relations know that there are no easy short cuts to long-term public approval. We know that the approach to favorable public opinion in the case of a corporation, for example, begins with the attitude of top management toward its employees, shareholders, the people in its community, its customers and the general public interest."

Now that we have perhaps gained some insight into what public relations is and what it is not and have explored some of the problems that are brought before the profession, it is clear that there are some attributes without which a person will find a career in public relations exceedingly difficult if not totally impossible.

I wish colleges had courses on orderly thinking, or just thinking, for that matter. Without the ability to think soundly, proper judgments are impossible and responsible decisions cannot be made. You'll be ahead of the game, too, if you have some writing ability, are creative, energetic, versatile and can work under pressure.

As to college training, most public relations executives favor a broad liberal arts curriculum. The subjects that are considered most useful are economics, English, psychology, the social sciences and creative writing, probably in that order. But whatever the order, a college education is clearly important, and the emphasis here is on "education" rather than "college."

I doubt if I ever realized it fully at the time, but my career in the field of news gathering was excellent basic training for a career in public relations. First as an associate editor of the *New York Journal of Commerce* and later as business editor of *Newsweek*, I learned to analyze a story, write it accurately and imaginatively (my supervisors would question these qualities from time to time) and work under the tremendous pressure of deadlines.

These are all essential parts of the public relations job and all public relations organizations are on the lookout for young men and women who possess these attributes.

It is hardly a coincidence that many of today's most successful public relations firms have staffs composed, in large measure, of former newsmen. Eighty-two percent of Hill and Knowlton's offers and account executives have backgrounds that included work on newspapers, wire services, magazines, radio and television.

While the principles of good public relations should be recognized by all who practice it—whether the company is small or is a corporate giant—the problems confronting the two are quite different. The public relations department of a local industry may have its share of problems, but they are localized in most cases, rarely extending beyond the borders of its community.

A firm that specializes in public relations, however, is not limited by geographical boundaries. Indeed, American business is increasing its international activity so rapidly that American businessmen are finding themselves increasingly entangled in a constant maze of government relations problems of the greatest complexity.

I have not been honest with you if I have conveyed the impression that the public relations business is like a perennial blue sky with no dark clouds. There are disadvantages and frustrations as in any other profession. Excellent programs, the result of many hours of hard work, are sometimes endlessly delayed or suddenly abandoned. Individual recognition may be slow and working hours are unpredictable.

But public relations men know that in the long run the disadvantages are offset by the frequent appearance of the unexpected challenge. Meeting these challenges is a stimulating adventure.

## 40

## SALES PROMOTION

*By* Roger A. Ross

It's a pet peeve of mine that many young writers completely neglect industry when looking for a position. They concentrate on the obvious sources of employment—newspapers, magazines, and advertising agencies. And year after year, profitable opportunities in industry are neglected.

I don't think there is any bias on the part of the young writer—I know there wasn't in my case. Most young men just don't realize that these jobs exist or how to go about finding them. There is also the problem of knowing they exist but not realizing that these positions offer the chance to do fascinating, different work with above-average personal and financial rewards.

It's no problem for me to tell you about writing at Smith, Kline & French Laboratories, but in order to give this article a little broader base to stand on and make it a little less like the world's longest placement ad, I reviewed the literature on the subject and talked to some knowledgeable people at a few other companies known to employ writers in interesting positions. So besides the specific things I say about a particular company, most of the observations I make will apply not only to SK&F but also to General Electric, Alcoa, and for that matter just about any company that does a significant amount of its own writing—rather than relying on outside specialists.

At SK&F, a writing career starts out with the writer development program. This is a flexible program designed to orient the individual to the drug industry in general, and SK&F in particular. Its length varies with the interests and abilities of the individual. Most young men and women who qualify are in the program for between 6 to 18 months.

During this time the participant is rotated through the various departments where writing is done. His duties consist of essentially the same things he would be doing in a permanent slot but with reduced responsibility and a little closer supervision. At the same time, the individual is offered a number of orientation experiences—formal and informal—in areas of the company directly related to the writing job, i.e. marketing research, sales, medical, international, etc.

The jobs for writers at SK&F are just about as varied as the number of writers employed, about a hundred. SK&F is one of several corporations in the U.S. which does all of its own advertising. This means that every magazine ad, direct-mail piece, and sales promotion item is written, designed and in many cases even printed right in the same building where research is carried out and the medicines are made.

In the Advertising and Sales Promotion Department, writers hold positions all along the chain of command. As an advertising and sales promotion writer, one gets a chance to create medical journal advertisements, direct-mail pieces, brochures for the nation's 180,000 practicing physicians, and sales promotion materials for the field force of over 500 men. In addition to creative copywriting, the job frequently involves conceiving strategy, planning campaigns, and design follow-through.

SK&F also employs writers in its General Promotion and its Medical Editing Departments. These are service oriented departments concerned with the production of magazines, pamphlets, exhibits, films, etc. which in general do not promote the sale of our products but rather are distributed to medical and paramedical professions as a service of the company.

A good example is *Consultant*, SK&F's medical journal. Each issue is composed of articles written by prominent physicians and edited and compiled by our own staff. Another magazine produced by SK&F is *Medical Assistant* (a quarterly magazine written for the 91,000 girls in the doctor's outer office).

Smith Kline & French also has an active Public and Industry Afairs Department whose writers prepare news releases and write speeches which are the voice of SK&F in its relations with the public and the pharmaceutical industry.

General Electric has a rather unique approach to the training of young writers. In general, G.E. is looking for men interested in the broad field of marketing who have specific talents in communications. Although the demands placed on a man accepted for the program extend beyond writing, this ability is nevertheless a key qualification. Evaluation of an applicant's writing talents is usually based on a tricky and demanding writing test unless a broad range of samples is available.

The program for young writers at G.E. best be characterized by saying that it is highly organized. It is a three-year program and each man is rotated through three one-year assignments in various phases of the work before going on to a permanent job.

At the same time, a graduate-level program of formal classes complements this work experience covering all phases of advertising from direct mail, space advertising, and press relations through motion picture, exhibits, research, and marketing. New courses are added as the need arises. Both the content and procedures of classes are periodically reviewed by recognized authorities from such schools as the Harvard Graduate School of Business Administration and Northwestern University's Medill School of Journalism.

Joseph W. Lovell, manager of G.E.'s Advertising Personnel Development Department is understandably enthusiastic about this comprehensive program. He feels that the program offers a uniquely thorough grounding in all phases of advertising and sales promotion to men who are capable of becoming the skilled professionals needed to plan and create effective and distinctive marketing communication programs.

G.E.'s Advertising and Public Relations Department employs about 500 people in jobs ranging from copywriting to script writing for motion pictures.

A good example of another approach to the training of young writers for positions in industry is the program of the Aluminum Company of America. At Alcoa, there is no formal classroom instruction. The new man has a specific assignment as part of the company's public relations staff. He receives his training, under the guidance of a skilled writer, through a great deal of practical experience and assignments.

After having tried training programs of a more formal nature in the past, Alcoa feels it gets more satisfactory results by hiring men for specific openings. Under this system, the writer applicant can be certain of the type of work he will be doing as an initial assignment, which is not the case in a rotation-type program.

This also means that Alcoa's standards for beginning writers are, if anything, more stringent than heretofore. According to William H. Shepard, manager of public relations for Alcoa, "the objective of our training program is not to teach people to write. We try to hire men and women who already have basic writing skills."

Alcoa has wide opportunities for writers in its organization. There are a dozen or so staff-written plant magazines, which offer typical starting jobs for new men. In the home office, beginning writers most frequently are hired to work on the company's national employee publication or in the product news area.

Writing is a prerequisite skill for all who are hired to fill vacancies in Alcoa's 50-man Public Relations Department. Writers in this department are involved in a wide range of activities, including such varied fare as preparing film strips, speeches, and television kits, and handling community and government relations programs. Alcoa's policy is to promote from within the company to fill its supervisory positions. Writing is no exception.

These are just a few examples of the opportunities that exist in industry for young writers. Today's corporations have a variety of audiences to reach—both inside and outside their companies. This means that in almost any field you can name there are firms who need writers to present their selling or service messages to these audiences.

The types of jobs are many, and the working conditions and financial rewards are generally very good. Most large companies are currently hiring writers with no experience at a starting salary of about $7,000 to $9,000 per year depending upon their level of education. Smaller corporations may pay less, but can usually offer a less formal working atmosphere.

The chances for advancement in an industrial writing position are surprisingly good. While not spectacular—like the oft referred to (but seldom documented) agency copywriter whose "dream campaign" sets the nation agog—the advancement is steady without the "make-or-break" quality. The result is usually longer tenure and more security.

Industry attracts people of many different types to fill its writing jobs. For example, I joined SK&F right out of Penn with a B.A. in psychology. One of my colleagues, Steve Goldstein, taught history for three years after graduating from Yale in 1961. One of the senior writers in our department, Jim Gould, originally came to SK&F because of its Design Department and his own interest in graphics. Today he combines both interests as a senior writer in the Advertising Sales Promotion Department.

These examples just serve to show that industrial writing careers can be satisfying and rewarding and that they appeal to people with a wide range of qualifications, backgrounds, and interests. I think you would do yourself a great disservice if you neglect to investigate the possibility of a writing career in industry. Check your placement office for leads; screen the current College Placement Annual; check newspapers for appropriate ads; send resumes to companies you're interested in (they may have several excellent writing jobs hiding under a bushel); in short, invest the little extra effort it takes to find out about these jobs. They are well worth the trouble. In no other market is there such a variety of positions and within them such a wide variety of responsibilities and assignments.

## 41

## THE BACKBONE OF RESEARCH

### By WILLIAM M. WEILBACHER

Advertising research brings new information and knowledge to the planning and creation of advertising. Advertising research provides understanding of how the advertising process achieves its objectives, economic and otherwise. It provides this new knowledge by actually doing original research or by summarizing, analyzing and interpreting the prior research of others.

Advertising research is perhaps most institutionalized in the advertising planning process. The post-World War II decades have been marked by a widespread increase of rationality in all business and this is both evidenced and reflected by a great deal more formal planning. Formal planning assumes formal intelligence. And the need for formal intelligence and data is, in fact, the need for research.

Before advertising is exposed to the public, some plan about how it will be exposed, to what degree, to whom, when, where, and with what objective must be developed. Advertising plans have become more rational, more formal and more visible in recent years, just as have all manner of other business plans. The need for advertising research has paralleled the increase in planning in advertising.

Perhaps there has been more emphasis on formal planning in advertising than in business generally. This may be so because the responsibility for advertising tends to fall or be divided between the advertiser's own advertising department, and the advertising agency. The advertiser's internal advertising department is usually expected to give direction and control to the advertising effort and the advertising agency is asked to provide the professional and executional talents required to produce finished advertising. (The agency is compensated for this activity, as a matter of custom, by a 15% commission allowed to it by the media which carry the finished advertising work plus or minus special "fee" arrangements between agency and client.)

In practice, it is difficult to keep the theoretically distinct activities of the advertising agency and the advertising department separate. The confusion in function frequently leads to a heightened need for formal planning, if only to make sure that the two organizations work well together and in a business-like way. The greater the pressure for formal planning, the greater the need for research.

Advertising research in the planning process is concerned with a great variety of issues: these are mostly related to where and how and why the advertising appropriation will be spent and whether, once spent, it has been successful. Here are some examples:

- What are the characteristics of the people who use the product? If they are women, for example, then the advertising plan must find ways to deliver the advertising messages to women.
- What are the dynamics of the purchase decision? Does the individual make his own decision, or is it made for him, or is it made jointly by him and other members of the family? Both advertising content and advertising placement will depend heavily, for example, upon whether the purchase decision is made by the individual (as in the case of cigarettes) or jointly by several family members (as in the case of refrigerators or automobiles) or is mixed decision (as in the case of electric shavers that are often bought by the male for himself, but as often, bought for him as a gift from other family members).
- How frequently are brand purchases made and what is the extent of brand loyalty over a series of purchases? Is the advertising objective, for example, to maintain loyal customers (as in packaged goods), or to encourage a substantial flow of new customers (as in the case of advertising for new homes), or both?
- What does the consumer use your product for, and under what kinds of circumstances? Does he use the product, for example, in all the ways it may be used, or only in a few, or in totally different ways, undreamt of by the designers? Dried onion soup mix is, for example, used both as a soup, and as an ingredient in cocktail dips.
- How does the consumer expose himself to advertising media and the advertising messages which they carry? What are the demographic characteristics, for example, of the individuals who read Life magazine or Playboy; of those who watch the Bonanza or Julia Child programs; of those who listen to baseball games or symphonic music; of those who drive their cars past outdoor posters or sit near the advertising in buses or subways? Which people, in which of these media audiences consume the product, when and how frequently?
- Has the advertising created awareness of, or favorable attitudes toward, or sales of, the product? Can the effects of the advertising expenditure be accounted for and with what degree of precision?

• All of these questions and many more have to do with advertising planning. Good answers to the questions (accurate, thorough, reasonable and timely) make for good advertising plans (better than those of the competitor, producing more sales and less expense). Advertising research has the responsibility of providing superior answers to such questions as a basis for superior advertising planning.

But there is more to advertising than planning. It is one thing to plan what will be done with the finished advertising and another to create the message to fill the plans.

How does advertising research contribute to the creative process, to the making of advertisements?

Much of the knowledge which underlies advertising plans is, of course, directly pertinent to the creation of advertising messages. But beyond this, advertising research has developed ways and means of developing knowledge that is especially relevant to creating superior advertising campaigns and advertisements.

And, even though advertising research capability is well advanced in this area, advertising research is less well accepted by the creative people than by their planning peers. Why is this so?

It is fashionable in some circles to say that advertising research cannot write advertisements. Sometimes the point is made in an even more extreme way and research is condemned as an inhibitor or restrictor of creative advertising solutions.

The researcher's point of view is that research extends the creative man's understanding of consumers. The creative man's only task is to create consumer knowledge, understanding, desire and/or conviction. Research extends the creative man's ability to accomplish this task. The notion of extension is in no way restrictive. It simply means that advertising research increases the creator's capability.

It is the essence of the creative process to take whatever is at hand and transform it for a particular purpose. The quality of the transformation reflects both the skill or genius of the creator and what he has to work with. The work of Gustav Mahler and Bob Dylan comes from exactly the same musical notes, yet with remarkably different results. So much for the contribution of the creator.

But, in advertising, the creators don't have to start even. Research can put more into the creator's hand and head as he *begins* his creative work. No man, as John Donne pointed out, is an island. This is particularly true of the advertising creator. But if the creator is not totally isolated, there are degrees of isolation. Advertising research is a contributor to non-isolation — a creator of new knowledge and understanding of the consumer. And, understanding of the consumer—his wants, his logic, his preceptions, his motives, his prejudices, his behavior, his opinions—all of these are grist for the creative man's mill. To deny the contribution of research is to affirm the necessity of isolation. One finds it hard to believe that this can be a propitious condition for the creator.

What kinds of questions does the advertising researcher address himself to in the creative sphere? Here are some examples:

- What role does the product play in the life of the consumer? What does the consumer expect from the product, and does it meet his expectations. If so, how? If not, why not? What kinds of communication content are most likely favorably to dispose the consumer to the product?
- What are the characteristics of the people who use the product, and those who do not? Is use or non-use a chance phenomenon, or are there reasonable and predictable bases for determining the incidence of use? Why are heavy users of the product, heavy users? Again, does heavy use seem to be unpredictable and random or does some rational framework underlie intensive product use.
- Do individual units of communication (magazine ads, television commercials) perform the tasks that they have been designed to do? How well or how poorly do they perform? Why do they perform as well or poorly as they do? How can they be improved? Should they be exposed to the consuming public at large?

All of these questions are addressed by research in the creative sphere.

We assert, then, that the role of research is to extend: to increase knowledge and understanding, and perhaps even to predict. How does the researcher work? What does he do? How does he spend his time? The advertising researcher is charged with two fundamental responsibilities: to identify what is unknown, and then to find ways of making the unknown, known.

A great deal of attention is paid to the researcher as a doer: as a finder out of unknowns. Thus, we think of the researcher immersed in tedious columns of figures, slide rule at the ready. We think of him as a writer of questionnaires; as a designer of complex sampling methods; as a deviser of subtle scales and psychological questioning procedures; as a director of complex computers; as, in summary, a data digger. And, it is true that the researcher is all of these things in his role as a producer of end research results.

But the conception of the researcher as an active gatherer of knowledge is too narrow for now, and dangerously limiting for the future. Increasingly, the important role of the researcher is to identify what is unknown, and from all the things that are unknown, what should be known. It is hard enough to know what one does know, without giving definition and structure to what one does not know. Yet this is the crucial role of the advertising researcher, for he must identify the key unknowns.

It has only been in the last ten or fifteen years that we have passed into the era of data glut. We now can find almost whatever facts we want to know. Data of all kinds abound, and the capability to get more data increases everyday. The problem increasingly is to determine what we need to know, or what it will be advantageous for us to know. We have too many facts at our disposal and too few means of identifying which are pertinent, and important.

In this sense, the advertising researcher works toward competitive advantage. If two equally capable creative people are working on essentially similar products with basically equal understanding of consumers, they will likely fall into some sort of competitive equilibrium if all other marketing (and economic factors) are equal.

The advertising researcher is concerned with identifying that knowledge of the consumer which will make it possible to develop or present one of these products so that it will be favorably appraised by consumers. To the extent that the researcher can point out specific knowledge of the consumer that is most likely to be decisive and where this knowledge is most likely to exist, a competitive advantage will be created which is as real as an advantage in production efficiency or efficiency in selling methods or any other business activity. The economic justification for such activity is clear when it is coupled with a clearly superior product characteristic. And, is it not difficult to argue that advertising created psychological satisfactions are lacking in benefit or value to the consumer who chooses to seek just such satisfactions? There are, after all, many grounds on which the consumer can be king.

As the advertising researcher probes for the bases of consumer acceptance and self-satisfaction, he merely reflects the point on the scale of developing taste and discernment that has been reached by the consumer of today. The process of advertising research must almost inevitably move the consumer positively along that scale as product modifications and bases for increased consumer satisfaction are identified, explored and pushed to fruition.

But what of the future? What kinds of problems will advertising research have to concern itself with in the next twenty years?

First, and always, the researcher will be concerned with the unfolding enigma of the consumer, as we have seen in the preceding paragraphs.

Second, the researcher will have to learn more about the dynamics of the advertising process. We do not yet know enough about how advertising works. No one yet can predict consistently or with high reliability which advertisements will be successful, and which will not.

Third, the researcher will have to discover ways of effectively communicating with consumers who are deluged with communication. The consumer is increasingly dazed by the proliferation of messages: informational, entertaining, advertising. How can advertising help to organize the consumer's communications world so that he is not sated by some aspects of it and undernourished by others?

These problems will certainly be in the minds of the men and women who enter the field of advertising research today. And there will be other problems, stimulating and challenging, that cannot be anticipated now. For the essence of advertising research is its diversity and unexpectedness. This quality is the hallmark of advertising research and it is the only one that will not change.